DATE DUE

Christian Faith and Man's Religion

CHRISTIAN FAITH AND MAN'S RELIGION

MARK C. EBERSOLE

THOMAS Y. CROWELL COMPANY

New York · Established 1834

ACKNOWLEDGMENTS

Acknowledgment is made to the following publishers for permission to quote from copyrighted material:

T. & T. Clark, Edinburgh, Scotland, for *The Christian Faith* by Friedrich Schleiermacher.

Harcourt, Brace & World, Inc., for *Scientific Method* by A. D. Ritchie.

Harper & Brothers, for *An Interpretation of Christian Ethics* by Reinhold Niebuhr, and for *The Word of God and the Word of Man* by Karl Barth, translated by Douglas Horton.

Holt, Rinehart and Winston, Inc., and Routledge & Kegan Paul, Ltd., London, for *Escape from Freedom* by Erich Fromm, copyright 1941 by Erich Fromm; and for *Man for Himself* by Erich Fromm, copyright 1947 by Erich Fromm; reprinted by permission of Holt, Rinehart and Winston, Inc., and Routledge & Kegan Paul, Ltd.

The Macmillan Company and Student Christian Movement Press Limited, London, for *Prisoner for God: Letters and Papers in Prison* by Dietrich Bonhoeffer, edited by Eberhard Bethge, translated by Reginald H. Fuller (New York: The Macmillan Company,

ACKNOWLEDGMENTS

1954; published by SCM Press under the title *Letters and Papers from Prison*).

Charles Scribner's Sons, for *Church Dogmatics* by Karl Barth, and for *The Nature and Destiny of Man* by Reinhold Niebuhr.

Student Christian Movement Press Limited, London, for *Dogmatics in Outline* by Karl Barth, translated by G. T. Thomson.

[v]

To Dorothy
and to Philip and Stephen

PREFACE

THIS BOOK is written primarily for those who want to learn something about Christian and religious thought of the modern era. It presents the ideas of several great thinkers and describes the general intellectual milieu within which their thought took shape. The study is focused upon the enigmatic question as to the relation of the Christian faith and man's religious consciousness. This question is a perennial one, of special and—one would expect—ineluctable concern to all persons who have, more or less, identified themselves with the Christian faith. The material presented in this volume is intended mainly for the beginning student rather than for the advanced scholar; it is exoteric rather than esoteric. There is no thought on the part of the author that the study will yield final answers, but it is hoped that the book will be suggestive, provoking the reader to further inquiry.

When one writes a book, John Donne's statement that "No man is an island, entire of itself" takes on a poignant relevance. For it was because of the critical advice and kindly acts of other persons that this study was undertaken and completed. I am indebted both to many of my colleagues at Bucknell University and to numerous friends elsewhere. A listing of all these persons is not possible, but the names of individuals to whom I am especially indebted dare not go unmentioned. Dr. Robert Gross, of the Department of English, read my entire manuscript and offered many helpful criticisms. His sympathetic interest, which was a constant source of encouragement, will never be forgotten. Mr. Harold Hayden, Librarian of Bucknell University, willingly made available the resources of the library and responded to my many inquiries and requests. Miss Marian Fister, my secretary, graciously refrained from exercising her right to complain about my indecipherable handwriting and never failed to maintain a good spirit throughout the tedious process of preparing the manuscript. Then, too, I owe a profound debt to the members of my family, who gave an existential relevance to the theology about which I was writing: our boys, Philip and Stephen, walking away dejected because their father did not give them the attention which they rightly deserved, made the idea of "judgment" disconcertingly vivid; my wife, Dorothy, giving herself unsparingly in every way in order that this book could be written, translated the idea of "love" into a reality.

M. C. E.

Bucknell University
Lewisburg, Pennsylvania

CONTENTS

1 Introduction   1

2 Religion Without the Christian Faith: Erich Fromm   19

3 The Christian Faith Without Religion: Dietrich Bonhoeffer   49

4 The Christian Faith as the Fulfillment of Religion: Friedrich Schleiermacher   79

5 The Christian Faith as the Judgment Against Religion: Karl Barth   105

6 The Christian Faith as the Judgment Against and the Fulfillment of Religion: Reinhold Niebuhr   133

7 Conclusion   163

Notes   185

Index   199

Christian Faith and Man's Religion

CHAPTER 1 Introduction

This book is a study in modern thought, investigating the nature of the Christian faith and man's religion, and the relation of the one to the other. What is the nature of faith? of religion? And to what extent do they duplicate or complement or obviate each other? Is there an essential difference between the two? Does the presence of the one preclude the presence of the other? Or are they compatible? Do they stand in a complementary or dialectical relation to each other? These are the questions around which the study revolves.

The discussions on the Christian faith and religion found in the five main chapters of this book represent ways whereby several influential thinkers have resolved this problem. That these particular points of view are not the only ones is, of course, obvious. What is intended here is simply to deal with some of the most representative ones; I have endeavored to include the extreme positions as well as some of the intermediate ones. Thus, the titles of the various chapters of the book are as follows: "Religion Without the Christian Faith: Erich Fromm"; "The Christian Faith Without Religion: Dietrich Bonhoeffer"; "The Christian Faith as the Fulfillment of Religion: Friedrich Schleiermacher"; "The Christian Faith as the Judgment Against Religion: Karl Barth"; "The Christian Faith as the Judgment Against and the Fulfillment of Religion: Reinhold Niebuhr." It should be clearly understood that the discussions contained in these five chapters do not represent an effort to delineate the whole span of the man's thought. The primary focus of the book is on the problem of the relation of the Christian faith to religion, and I have simply attempted to present those aspects of the man's thought which provide a discussion of this subject.

Not a few Christians—both clergy and laity—will be perplexed by the subject of this book: What is the relation of the Christian faith to religion? Is not this question sheer equivocation? they will ask. After all, the Christian faith and religion are synonymous and the terms are, therefore, interchangeable. "A rose by any other name would smell as sweet." In their opinion, there is no issue. They assume that if one discards the traditional practices and forms of Christianity, he has thereby shed all vestiges of religion. And the converse is also believed true. They are inclined to equate religious strivings with the concerns peculiar to the Christian faith, the assumption being that the content and spirit of the former is no different from that of the latter. And, of course, it is true that one can advance a cogent argument that the Christian faith and religion are substantially one and the same thing. Yet, this more sophisticated effort to equate Christianity with religion is quite unlike the indiscriminate habit of lumping the two together.

Generally speaking, the widespread practice among Christians, as well as other persons, of equating the one with the other is evidence of an exceedingly fuzzy understanding of the Christian faith. And, as is to be expected, this undistilled and ambiguous perspective is not without serious consequences. It serves to bring dishonor to the Christian faith, prompting people both to reject hastily and to embrace prematurely all that is associated with it.

Thus, the first matter at hand is to clarify the meaning of the terms *religion* and *Christian faith*. Religion has been defined in a variety of ways, each definition bearing its own peculiar nuance. And it is not likely that there will soon arise a court which will settle the issue for all time. The discussion and debate about the elusive term *religion* is bound to continue. Throughout this study the assumption is that religion is tantamount to seriousness, to being "ultimately concerned" about one's life. The religious person is one who is serious about life —about finding meaning for his life. According to Lactantius, the word *religion* is derived from the verb *religare,* which means "to rebind"; in other words, to be religious is to be "bound" or to be "possessed" by something. Or to put it differently, religion is "involvement"; to be deeply involved in one's existence is to be religious.

But the question arises, where does God come into the picture? Can one be religious without a God? Is the atheist religious? God, according to the above definition, is that which one conceives to be ultimately important; it is that object which gives meaning to one's life. For Moses, God is Yahweh; for the "rich young ruler," God is wealth and prosperity; for Mohammed, God is Allah; for John Dewey, God is "the unity of all ideal ends arousing us to desire and actions." The term *religion* cannot be reserved for the theistical point of view. Indeed, if this were the case, original Buddhism and Jainism could not be regarded as religions, since they are without an objective reality called God. The term *religion* is all-embracing, running the gamut from absolute theism to the extreme forms of atheism. Communism is—as Berdyaev and many other persons have pointed out—intensely religious. For the Communist, the state is all-important; it is the state which commands one's loyalties and sustains one's being. Will Herberg, in discussing some of the "substitute faiths of our time," says of Marxism: ". . . its appeal has been almost entirely religious: it has offered modern man an absolutist faith, a world-view in which the cosmic force of the Dialectic is seen as realizing the ends and sustaining the values that give meaning to life." He then goes on to say, "To the believer who, through his belief, aligns himself with the 'movement of History,' it grants the feeling of security and self-esteem that comes from identification with omnipotent power as well as the confidence that is the result of the assurance of ultimate victory. In this sense, Marxism is one of the most potent religions of modern times." [1] What Herberg says about the religion of communism is equally true about any other "godless" system or object which commands man's uncondi-tional loyalty.

Thus, the nonreligious person (if there is such a person) is not an atheist; instead, he is one who does not take life seriously, one who is not deeply concerned about the meaning of his life. He is not possessed by any "reality" or "cause," either within or without himself; he is not involved in any real concern. The nonreligious person is one who is without a god; for him there is no Yahweh, no living for wealth, no Allah, no "unity of ideal

[1] Notes will be found at the end of the book.

[4]

ends." He drifts, indifferent and unconcerned. Is not Kierkegaard alluding to a nonreligious attitude when he writes about the spiritless Christian within Christendom? This person, explains Kierkegaard, "goes to church every Sunday, hears and understands the parson, yea, they understand one another; he dies; the parson introduces him into eternity for the price of ten dollars—but a self he was not, and a self he did not become." [2]

Or, again, one is reminded of several incidents in Leo Tolstoy's "The Death of Ivan Ilych." The blasé way in which various persons witness the death of Ivan Ilych suggests the nonreligious spirit. Ivan had died—a kind of misfortune from which, they assumed, they were eternally divorced. And upon learning of Ivan's death, they, writes Tolstoy, "could not help thinking . . . that they would now have to fulfill the very tiresome demands of propriety by attending the funeral service and paying a visit of condolence to the widow." And upon visiting the house where Ivan's body was lying, one of the friends, Schwartz, takes time to wink at his colleague, Peter Ivanovich, "as if to say 'Ivan Ilych has made a mess of things —not like you and me.'" [3] Illustrations could be multiplied, but the point here is evident: if a person's life were characterized by such a lighthearted, uninvolved, unconcerned attitude, one could rightly conclude that such a person was nonreligious.

Paul Tillich's definition of religion goes to the heart of the matter. To be religious, says Tillich, is to be unconditionally concerned. The individual has an infinite passion and interest in his existence; he encounters reality with an ultimate concern. Religion is not confined to church and doctrinal statements; it includes all expressions of unconditional concern, both secular and nonsecular. Religion, for Tillich, is the concern about one's being and nonbeing. "The religious concern," he writes, "is ultimate; it excludes all other concerns from ultimate significance; it makes them preliminary. The ultimate concern is unconditional, independent of any conditions of character, desire, or circumstances. The unconditional concern is total: no part of ourselves or of our world is excluded from it; there is no 'place' to flee from it." [4] To be "ultimately concerned" about one's existence is to be religious.

Granted that religion is best defined as "seriousness" or "ultimate concern," what is meant by the term *Christian faith?* Here again we are confronted with a very ambiguous and evasive term. Under the rubric of the Christian faith all sorts of theological ideas and systems have been promulgated. Indeed, this is precisely the problem before us. Since the time of the Enlightenment—and before, for that matter—various interpretations of the Christian faith have been set forth, each one claiming to express the essence of the gospel. Obviously, at this point our definition of the Christian faith cannot be a normative one, although, at the end of the study, such a definition will be suggested. At best, we must presently settle for a preliminary statement regarding the nature of the Christian faith. Such a statement is required so that, in the discussion which follows, it will be evident that, even though the Christian faith may be inextricably related to religion, the former must not *ipso facto* be equated with the latter. It must be made clear that, in a generic sense, Christianity has certain elements which distinguish it from religion. Thus, keeping in mind that the preliminary definition must both point to the peculiar elements

[6]

of the Christian faith, and be sufficiently inclusive to embrace the various points of view which are presented in the ensuing chapters, I suggest that there are at least three elemental beliefs which are characteristically Christian.

For one thing, according to the Christian faith man belongs to God. He is a creature of God, a child of God. For man to bestow his allegiance and devotion upon any reality or being other than God is to abandon his true "creatureliness." "The Christian doctrine of creation," to use J. S. Whale's words, "is a symbolic assertion . . . that man in all his felt finitude comes from God and goes to God: he is not surrounded by a sheer abyss of nothingness. God . . . is the ground and goal of all that is. All is of God—our creation, preservation and all the blessings of this life; the redemption of the world, the means of grace and the hope of glory." [5] It is before God that every knee should bow and every man confess that He is the Lord. It is through him that "we live and move and have our being." Man belongs not to principalities or angels or demons or to any other creature; he belongs exclusively to God. To know this God and to abide by His will—this, claims the Christian faith, is the chief end of man.

The central figure of Christianity is Christ. He is the norm and catalyst of man's life, representing to man that which is good and true—representing God. According to the Christian faith, it is Christ who is the center around which man's life is oriented, judged, and reconciled. Christ is regarded as the manifestation of the Kingdom of God, revealing to man the way of peace and reconciliation. Christ is looked upon as the way of truth and life, causing men to mend their ways and to seek the more nearly perfect way. Christ directs men to God; He is the "light of the world" in that He points to the divine light.

Through Christ, God is represented as one who is infinitely loving. God is not a being who has removed Himself from the exigencies and strivings of man; He is greatly concerned about the life of man, speaking to man and ordering his life. Christ points to the God who loves all men—the sinner and the saint, the outcast and the aristocrat. And because God loves all men, men ought always to love one another. Indeed, there are no greater laws than these: "Thou shalt love the Lord thy God with all thy heart, soul and mind and strength; and thou shalt love thy neighbor as thyself. Upon these laws hang all the law and the prophets." Love is the law of all life. It is in love that man's crooked ways are made straight and that man comes to the full realization of his being. Christians may disagree as to whether the divine love involves primarily man and man, or man and God, or both of these, but they are united in the affirmation that the God of whom Christ speaks is one of infinite compassion, sending rain upon the just and the unjust (although Fromm would conclude that the authoritarianism of Christianity yields a very loveless life).

The terms are now defined: *Religion* refers to man's "serious," "ultimate" concern about the meaning of his existence; the *Christian faith* denotes the affirmation that man belongs to God, and that Christ, the representative of the divine, is the central figure of man's life, instilling within man the awareness that God is a god of love.

Although the scope of the book is limited to the modern era, the subject it treats is not unique to modern times. During the past two thousand years persons from both inside and outside the Christian Church have given consideration to this matter, in one way or another. We recall, for instance, Celsus, who denounced the Christian faith, contending that the authentic proprietors of truth were the Greeks; Clement and Origen, who argued that the Logos of Christ is not radically different from the logos of man; Tertullian, who insisted that Jerusalem has nothing to do with Athens; and one could go on to mention Augustine, Aquinas, Luther, and many others. The point is, the issue is an old one—as old as the Christian Church.

At the same time, the problem of relating the Christian faith to religion as it is dealt with in the modern era is not without a unique quality. And what this quality is can be explained in this manner. The term *modern era* refers to the time from the Enlightenment to the present day. That the Enlightenment marks the beginning of the modern era is a generally conceded fact, since it represents Western man's departure from the medieval world-view and the introduction of the view of a brave new world—the world in which we still live today. "This eighteenth-century view of life," writes Crane Brinton, "though modified in the last two centuries, is still at bottom *our* view of life, especially in the United States." [6] In the name of the Enlightenment, the antiquated medieval way of looking at life was forced to capitulate to a more modern frame of reference. The enlightened mind shook the very foundation of historic Christianity. Thus, the Christian was forced to re-examine his faith and to recast it in new forms. Old things had passed away. Man had gone modern, and there was no turning back. Crane Brinton summarizes this point by reminding us that "The American fundamentalist driving his Ford through Mencken's 'Bible Belt' cannot be what his sixteenth-century predecessor was, if only because he is driving a Ford—and may live to see his son drive a Lincoln." [7]

Thus it is that our study of the Christian faith and religion in its modern setting must be seen against the background of the Enlightenment's vigorous attack against historic Christianity. The nature of this conflict is, as everyone knows, a long and complicated story—men fought for a variety of reasons and with various degrees of intensity. Yet, in the main, it is evident that the encounter revolved around certain fundamental issues. Put in its broadest terms, the cause of conflict was the contention of the enlightened minds that the gravity of all life must be shifted "from the Christian supernatural heaven after death to the rationalist natural heaven on this earth, now—or at least very shortly." [8] More specifically, it can be said that there were at least three basic issues at stake. For one thing, the spokesmen of the Enlightenment argued that the world would steadily "progress," so that mankind could with confidence anticipate an inexorable march toward perfection. Why were they so assured that the days ahead would be bright? Because, came the reply, the rationality of man is written into the very fiber of his being; he is, above all else, a rational being. And since "progress is due to the spread of reason, to the increasing enlightenment," man can be certain that human power will be harnessed, to the end that the world will become better and better.

But this "secular" eschatology stood in opposition to the historic Christian canons and traditions. The perfect life is, according to the medieval theologians, a transcendental miracle, brought about only by a sovereign being. Everything, it

was asserted, depends upon an almighty god who can inter-
vene within history at his good pleasure and who holds within
his hands the destiny of all men. It is God who rules, not man;
salvation is celestial bliss, not terrestrial progress. The positions
of the Enlightened and the Christians appeared to be mutually
exclusive.

Then, too, for eighteenth-century men the only medium
through which both nature and man could be adequately
analyzed and synthesized was human reason. The Christian
idea of revelation, they argued, is sheer nonsense. It stultifies
the human mind, putting a premium on ignorance and en-
couraging the blind approbation of Biblical superstitions. The
leaders of the new thought were certain that a faith predicated
upon revelation could yield nothing but absurd creeds and
silly doctrines. Some of the less sophisticated rationalists of
the century went so far as to insist that aside from the detri-
mental effects of the idea of revelation much of the falsity
of the Christian tradition could be traced to "priestly villainy,"
"deliberate charlatanry," and the "conspiracy to fool the innocent many." What an inane business Christianity is! The
credulity which is so highly prized by the Christian faith inevitably serves to destroy man's most precious gift of reason,
charged the propagators of modern thought. So it was that the
men of the Enlightenment set out to demolish the authority of
revelation in favor of the final word of reason.

And, quite naturally, accompanying the faith in progress
and reason was the eighteenth-century belief that man is good.
Man is "sound and sensible," and, barring any unnatural in-
terruptions, he will follow the counsel of his innate wisdom.
By what empirical evidence does the Christian faith berate

[11]

man, regarding him as a vile and perverse creature? Certainly it is true that man does make mistakes and is at times somewhat maladjusted, but only an uninitiated mind would conclude that man is therefore wicked, or "born in sin." Man is by nature good, which is to say that he is fully equipped to live creatively in his physical and social environment. Christianity is, insisted the leaders of the Enlightenment, doing a gross injustice to human nature when it interprets man's life according to the imaginary fall in Genesis. Actually, man is a free, enterprising being, whose basic fiber is saturated with the highest ambitions and whose mind is capable of reflecting true knowledge. The enlightened rationalists required that the Christians, once and for all, surrender their anachronous notion regarding the depravity of man.

The battle between the spirit of the Enlightenment and the tradition of Christianity was truly a conflict between two different world-views—and two different schemes of salvation. Christianity affirmed that God had created all that is, and that, while man was created good, Adam, in defying God, brought sin upon mankind. Thus it is that all men are miserable offenders. Yet, there is a way out: the grace of God and, in some instances, a measure of good works, compounded with true contrition, can deliver man from his dreadful plight. The path to the bliss of heaven is straight and narrow, but all who repent and believe may enter therein. Undergirding this entire scheme of salvation is—as the Enlightened saw it—a fierce threat that anyone who has offended the Almighty God will eventually have to face a final reckoning—a reckoning which will send the vicious to hell and the virtuous to heaven; the combination of the authority of God and the dreadful fear

[12]

of losing one's soul drove men to a desperate search for salvation.

It is primarily this Christian scheme of things which the Enlightenment sought to alter, if not destroy. The argument was that the presuppositions upon which the Christian world is predicated are false and imaginary. The world must not be explained as the creation of a personal, loving god; rather, it must be viewed as the outcome of the operations of a vast machine called "nature." And all the talk about the soul's ascending to heaven or descending to hell after death must be repudiated. When the machine stops, the total life of man disintegrates so that the Christian idea of eternal life is sheer fantasy. And guilt— What actually is it? It is nothing other than the sense of right and wrong of the human conscience, which emerges out of man's interaction with his environment. Man must be made free and happy, unhampered by the many nonsensical qualms imposed upon him by the idea that there is a god who watches and judges his thoughts and actions, one to whom he must some day give an account of himself. In place of the paralyzing schemes of Christianity, man must work out his destiny, and, surely, by relying upon his own inherent sagacity, he will point the way toward, and design the program for, the fulfillment of his life.

This is a simple—and somewhat exaggerated—description of the points at which the Enlightenment clashed with historic Christianity. In every way, the two movements seemed to be at cross purposes, and it is this conflict which provides the background for this study. For the eighteenth century's challenge to traditional faith constitutes the matrix within which the modern discussion regarding the relation of the Christian faith to religion must be considered. The men of the Enlightenment set forth their point of view with such a tremendous impact that the men of faith were constrained to re-examine and redefine the nature of this position: the new naturalism threatened to destroy the supernaturalism of Christianity. In the face of the Enlightenment how was the Christian faith to be delineated? This was the crucial issue.

Only one last preliminary matter remains: to what extent does our subject have any real relevance to the life of the "average" Christian? Certainly it is a travesty on truth to imagine that the subject is of interest only to the theologian. In other words, our topic is not—as the popular saying goes—"simply a theological issue." On the contrary, it is decidedly—indeed, poignantly—relevant. And the fact of its relevance becomes plainly evident if we observe one of America's most recent phenomena: her "religious resurgence."

During the past ten years or more, religion enjoyed an unprecedented popularity in America. Among its leading spirits and most revered voices was President Dwight D. Eisenhower, who publicly embraced the Christian faith and who repeatedly advised his fellow countrymen of the indispensable place of "faith"; the Reverend Billy Graham, who "crusaded" in America's large cities and convinced thousands of people of their need for "salvation"; and the Reverend Norman Vincent Peale, who instructed the nation in the practicality of the Christian faith and its ability to produce a healthy-happy-confident-successful life. Both in and out of season, religious topics and practices were acclaimed as being pre-eminently important, and the many endeavors designed to enhance man's spiritual welfare were heartily lauded and widely appropriated. Leading personalities of stage and screen, eminent statesmen and politicians, famous athletes and sportsmen—these and many other persons felt constrained to issue testimonies of belief. From every quarter of the country, the worthy aims and noble consequences of the spiritual life were roundly sounded.

Concomitantly, as the revival flourished, a sharp controversy ensued as to its validity and ultimate meaning. Pulpits were loud and magazines were heavy with judgments, both pro and con. Many Americans viewed the religious resurgence with deep satisfaction, hoping that it would continue to grow. "Why not?" they asked. The churches are filled every Sunday; more religious books are being published than ever before; movies based on Biblical narratives are box-office hits; Madison Avenue jockeys are spinning spiritual discs; and the United States government has officially acknowledged that this nation is "under God." Why should not this high spiritual fervor merit man's endorsement and God's benediction? Why should anyone question its merit? The Reverend Edward L. R. Elson vouched for the genuineness of the spiritual affairs within the nation's capital; Vice-President Richard Nixon traveled to Yankee Stadium to give his blessing to Dr. Graham's crusade in New York City; Dr. Daniel A. Poling, Mr. Grove Patterson (a newspaper editor), and countless others expressed appreciation for the ministry of Dr. Peale.[9]

On the other hand, a minority group within the country viewed the revival with a degree of apprehension. Some members offered mild correctives, but many more issued hard and caustic denunciations. The religious resurgence of the nation, they argued, is little or nothing more than the supplanting of the Judeo-Christian tradition with a phony religiosity. In essence, they contended, the movement represents the utilization of God as a means of realizing personal ambitions; it misunderstands and recoils from the social demands of the gospel; and it glorifies "faith" and "religion" rather than God. Among the most forthright critics were some of the country's leading preachers and teachers: Bishop G. Bromley Oxnam declared that in some cases religion "is being identified with a cult of success, and prayer is but a means to promotion to the presidency of the company." [10] Professor Will Herberg contended that "the religiousness characteristic of America today is very often a religiousness without religion . . . a way of sociability or 'belonging' rather than a way of reorienting life to God." [11] Professor William L. Miller averred that the resurgence fosters "religiosity," not "orthodoxy," and that it perpetuates faith in "our own worshipping," "not in God." [12]

But our immediate interest is not to review the entire verbal skirmish that took place—this has already been done by Will Herberg, by Roy Eckhart, and by others. Our concern is only to point out that at the very heart of the nationwide controversy was precisely the issue that is treated in this study: What is the relation of the Christian faith to religion? Unfortunately, as the controversy continued, the real issue was not infrequently smothered by the heat generated by the polemics. Much of the debate was inflamed by the hurling of clichés and labels, the use of ambiguous terms, and the enunciation of categorical indictments without any effort to disclose the presuppositions upon which they were predicated. One had to penetrate this level of the debate to get to the heart of the matter. The question which was really at stake was this: did the contemporary religious "revival" represent an authentic expression of the Christian faith, or was it nothing more than a manifestation of the ideals and ambitions which spring from man's natural religious concern about the meaning of his existence? Did the religious interest contain those elements which are truly at the heart of the gospel, or was it simply a case of employing the traditional Christian terms to provide a sanction for the aspirations of the human (all too human) spirit? To put the matter succinctly, in the postwar resurgence of religion in America, was man worshiping God or was he worshiping man? This is the heart of the problem.

Thus, the discussion in this book represents an effort to help illuminate a problem that is not simply a concern of the clergy and the scholar but one that is of crucial importance to every Christian. The particular historical circumstances out of which this issue arises will, of course, vary from age to age. At one time the situation may be the "religious resurgence" of the 1950's; at another time it may be the "social gospel" or the "great awakening" or "empiricism" or "orthodoxy" or some other response which has a significant bearing upon the spiritual welfare of the people. Whatever the nature of the times, the relation of faith to religion is a perennial concern and one which directly affects the life of the Christian.

CHAPTER 2 Religion Without the Christian Faith: Erich Fromm

ERICH FROMM *was born in Germany, in Frankfurt, in 1900. He studied sociology and psychology at the universities of Heidelberg, Frankfurt, and Munich. He earned his Ph.D. degree from the University of Heidelberg and was trained in psychoanalysis in Munich and later at the Psychoanalytic Institute in Berlin. Since 1925 he has given himself to his psychoanalytical practice and his theoretical work. He first came to America in 1933 to lecture at the Chicago Psychoanalytical Institute. One year later he became a citizen of the United States, and since that time he has taught at such schools as Bennington College, Columbia University, and Yale University and at a number of institutes of psychiatry. In addition to publishing various works while in Germany he has become well known for the books that he has written since he has come to this country. Among the works written during the latter period are* ESCAPE FROM FREEDOM (*1941*), MAN FOR HIMSELF (*1947*), PSYCHOANALYSIS AND RELIGION (*1950*), THE ART OF LOVING

(1956). Certainly it cannot be denied that Fromm is one of the most influential humanistic voices in contemporary America.

FROM DR. ERICH FROMM, one of the most prominent psychoanalysts and social philosophers of our day, comes a pronouncement of this nature: Religion comes to its proper fruition not through the aegis of some authoritative agent but through the exercise of human intelligence and will. Man need not look outside of himself for help—it is a matter of "man for himself." Man, by his very nature, possesses sufficient power and wisdom to cope with life; he can himself discover the good and the evil and through his own strivings can realize the conditions essential for his well-being. The superhuman beings and supernatural agents traditionally identified with the religious life are unnecessary; what is more, they are menacing imposters in the human domain and a denial of human dignity and freedom. More specifically, the Christian faith with its Almighty God and its exhortation that man prostrate himself before this Omnipotent Power is blatantly inimical to human maturity and happiness. Christianity perpetuates the baneful view that man is nothing more than a means, an instrument to be manipulated according to the pleasures of an omnipotent deity; it maintains that man must sacrifice himself in order that the Almighty God's craving for glory and sweet savor may be satisfied. In essence, the Christian faith is an authoritarian gospel that is unmistakably negative and that eventuates in the destruction of human personality. Man's high dignity and rightful felicity can be realized only through man himself or, more explicitly, through a humanistic ethics which completely excludes the authoritarianism of the Christian faith.

The point of view that Fromm is expressing reflects the spirit of the eighteenth-century Enlightenment. Like the humanists of the Enlightenment, Fromm stakes his case upon the powers and capacities of man. Man can know the truth apart from supernatural revelation, and he can live the good life without superhuman grace, declare the prophets of the eighteenth century. Glory be to man; he is to be trusted; he is the judge of all truth and the author of all virtue. Let people everywhere renounce their dependence upon divine authority; let them be free from the shackles of ecclesiastical powers and from the bonds of traditional doctrines. They insist that it is time that the individual take his full measure. He must—if he is to realize his true destiny—assert his autonomy, regain his self-confidence, rely upon his own intellectual acumen and achievements. In general, this was the humanistic faith upon which Fromm constructed his gospel of "man for himself." More specifically, there are at least three basic tenets of the Enlightenment which, because of their bearing upon Fromm's thought, should be given particular attention.

First, declare the voices of the Enlightenment, man is fundamentally good. Jean Jacques Rousseau stoutly and convincingly maintains that man is by nature good, that evil is the result of deficient teaching and institutions. Robert Owen stalwartly defends the virtue of man by insisting that the source of all evil is attributable to the environment. In the minds of the eighteenth-century thinkers, the Christian notion that in the Garden of Eden man fell into a state of depravity is sheer imagination and nonsense. The truth is that man is good—that man is competent to master his own fate. Granted the proper use of his intellectual faculties, it is argued, man can become whatever he wants to become.

Helvetius, although at times a bit extreme in his point of view, does not fail to reflect the humanistic spirit when he insists that man hold within his hands the instruments for greatness and happiness, and that the realization of these ideal states is primarily a matter of perfecting the science of education. Helvetius has unlimited faith in the ability of the skillful and sagacious leader to mold the character of men and to bring about the millennium for wise and peaceful citizens. The moral fiber of man is not bent toward perversity, says the spokesman of the Enlightenment. If the mind of man is sufficiently illuminated, man will respond to his world in a most appropriate and honorable manner. Thus, mankind can rightly look forward to the bright and glorious days of the future. Voltaire, too, is vigorous in his declaration that reason and industry will surely improve, that the evils which afflict men will gradually disappear. He is convinced that the world in which he lives has ushered in the age of reason and that now, with this power at man's command, it is a foregone conclusion that the course of mankind will move steadily upward.

Condorcet subscribes to essentially the same optimistic view. He believes that no limits can be set to the improvement of the human faculties, that "the perfectibility of man is absolutely indefinite." And, concerning the specific forms which human progress will take, Condorcet joins in the views of others by explaining that man will progress in terms of the realization of equity between nations as well as within nations and that there will eventuate a "real improvement in man." All in all, many men of the Enlightenment harbor the belief that the events of mankind must be viewed as a march of progress, that man is so constituted that in time the gap between man's potential existence and his fulfilled existence will be bridged; the perfect life is clearly within the bounds of earthly and human possibility. These declarations of progress are, in effect, paeans in praise of man, of the ineffaceable goodness of man, and of the great heights upon which man will eventually stand.

A second tenet—and a corollary to the idea of the goodness of man—is the assertion of faith in reason and, more particularly, in the scientific method. By virtue of the fact that man is good, it naturally follows that man is reasonable. The eighteenth century, in overthrowing the authority of revelation and the Church, endows science with final authority. The story of how this shift of power came about is a long and complicated one, and it is beyond our present concern. But there is one fact which is particularly germane at this point —the fact that the scientific method became the instrument for knowing not only the natural world but the human world as well. The eighteenth century was the heir of the Newtonian science. The eminent Sir Isaac Newton, relying upon the findings of his predecessors, formulated the scientific scheme for the examination and explanation of the physical world—the solar system, gravity, mass, and everything else in this category. His method was, to begin with, to analyze observed facts, and then proceed to deduce a basic principle, then to deduce a mathematical consequence of this principle, and then, through experimentation, to prove that what followed from the principle was in agreement with experience. But the method can be learned later. What is to be remembered now is that Newton, by devising the scientific method, was able to account for the material universe without recourse to a loving and creating god, thereby delivering a severe blow to orthodox Christianity.

But the story of science does not end here. Having conquered the physical world, science goes on to invade the human world. Observing the operation of Newton's ideas upon the physical universe, some persons conclude that there is no reason why the method of science is not applicable to the understanding of man. Looking back over history, one may well conclude that the "science of man" is actually the eighteenth century's highest claim to fame. John Locke, among others, puts forth a scientifically grounded account of man. With the image of Newtonian science fresh in his mind, he proceeds to analyze human nature to discover its component parts. Reporting his findings, he announces that all ideas are a product of experience and of reflections on experience—i.e., of *sensations* and *reflections*. Apart from these two sources, he says, there can be no gaining of knowledge. Locke himself was not exactly an irreligious person, but his empirical basis for understanding man constitutes an attack on the Christian faith. What he is saying is that all religion must be founded upon reason, upon the insights gained through experience—an attitude which means, obviously, that there is no place for divine revelation. All knowledge begins with man, with an understanding of what man is, and all ideals—philosophical, political, or whatever—must be in keeping with the natural "laws" and natural "propensities" of human nature. It is Locke's idea that the guideposts for human existence must be erected by the science of man rather than by the revelation of the Church. And it is this idea which is so enthusiastically appropriated by the enlightened minds of the eighteenth century.

Another major tenet of the Enlightenment is the notion that the moral ideals by which man lives issue from man himself. The principles of right and wrong are, it is claimed, matters that are resolved through science and reason, ethics being as independent of supernatural foundations as is any other branch of human knowledge. In rather resounding tones, the eighteenth-century thinkers contend that just as the laws of the physical world and of man are known through the study of the "natural," so the principles of the good life have a natural origin. It is argued that to know what man is, is to know what man ought to be; the order of nature contains the order of the natural moral law as well. The good is equated with the natural. This means that the question is not, What doth the Lord require of me? but rather, What doth Nature disclose to me? The traditional religious sanctions are dropped, and men are advised to stop worrying about God. Nature is regarded as a reliable basis for human conduct. A vigorous plea is made for a "religion of reason, a system of ethics without all the nonsense of theology." The ideas of Alexander Pope do not necessarily enjoy universal acclaim, yet there is widespread approval of his affirmation that

> All Nature is but art, unknown to thee;
> All chance, direction, which thou canst not see;
> All discord, harmony not understood;
> All partial evil, universal good:
> And, spite of pride, in erring reason's spite,
> One truth is clear, Whatever is, is right.

Intoxicated by the glorification of the natural order the naturalistic philosophers set forth their ethical systems. Among the most well-known systems are those of David Hume and Jeremy Bentham. Hume develops a theory of ethics based on the idea of subjective sympathy. He agrees with Pope: "Whatever is, is right"; and, from this premise, he goes on to conclude that pleasure and pain are the foundations of value judgments. His logic is this: because man enjoys a feeling of pleasure when he loves and serves his fellow men, such behavior should be called *good;* because man experiences the feeling of pain when he injures others, such behavior should be called *evil.* Implicit in this reasoning is the belief that, since a sense of satisfaction issues from befriending others, it is natural for man to identify himself sympathetically with his friends and fellow countrymen. There may be limitations to the extent of his sympathy; nevertheless, the fact remains that it is the natural sympathy of man which is the basis of the moral life.

Bentham, too, believed that morality is founded upon human nature. Thus arise the questions: What is the nature of man? What are his needs, his desires? Bentham argues that what man wants above all else is to secure pleasure and to avoid pain. Here, then, is the basis for ethics: the individual's desire for happiness naturally leads him to desire the greatest happiness for the largest number of people. All conduct must be measured in terms of its ability to produce happiness and all human enterprises must be devoted to the realization of this moral ideal. The task of the moralist is to determine what general principles will bring about the greatest number of pleasures and the least number of pains. The obligation of the lawmaker is to enact legal measures which will yield true happiness.

Hume and Bentham, in keeping with eighteenth-century humanism, are dedicated to the proposition that all morality is grounded in man and that ethics can get along very well without God—especially the God of Christianity.

The above delineation of the Age of Reason is not intended to be a complete account of what happened during this great era; the magnitude and variation of the thought of the period go far beyond what has been described. The material presented has been designed simply to indicate three of the great ideas of the Enlightenment which seem to be most relevant to the humanistic emphasis contained in the thought of Erich Fromm. That Fromm was a child of the Enlightenment appears to be an indisputable fact. His entire thesis regarding the nature of man and his prescription for the realization of man's well-being clearly reflect the eighteenth-century spirit. Like the men of the Enlightenment, he believes that the good life —the realization of the self—becomes a reality through the conjuring of the *human spirit* rather than through the supplication of the *Holy Spirit*. Man is so constituted that he can and ought to go it alone. In fact, there is no real alternative.

In Fromm's own discussion of the humanistic tradition he provides a résumé of the thought of some of the most outstanding philosophers and acknowledges his debt to them. In his presentation of the thought of these men, it is Spinoza's philosophy, as much as any, which illustrates most vividly Fromm's indebtedness to eighteenth-century thought. Spinoza, as Fromm interprets his thought, develops a system of ethics which is completely naturalistic. The Dutch philosopher claims that man has a natural desire to preserve his being and to realize his essential nature. What this fact means is that man desires above all else to come nearer and nearer to the model of human nature. Man wants to become as "fully human" as possible. Thus, explains Fromm, *virtue* for Spinoza is the realization of the potentialities inherent within man; it is the process of becoming "more human." Conversely, *evil* must be conceived of all that which impedes man's realization of his "humanness." No god is needed to instruct man concerning good and evil. Goodness is the realization of man's nature, and it is through reliance upon human intelligence that the nature of man is discerned. But Fromm's indebtedness to Spinoza as well as his allying himself with the intellectual movement of the eighteenth century will become apparent only as his thought is examined more closely.

At the outset of the consideration of Fromm's thought it should be noted that he takes seriously man's predilection to be religious; he asserts unequivocally that religion is at the heart of human existence. In making this claim he does not use the term *religion* because, as he explains, of its common association with a theistic rather than an atheistic system. In place of the term *religion* he recommends the phrase "frames of orientation and devotion." Yet, whatever the semantics, the fact remains that Fromm is averring that man is religious and that religion is a phenomenon peculiar to all human existence.

Religion, Fromm explains, is tantamount to the search for the meaning of life. The need to find unity and equilibrium, to make sense out of human existence, is inescapable; it springs from the depths of man's being. Unlike the animal, man is not content simply to gratify the physical drives of hunger, thirst, and sex; the human being must strive for something beyond the attainment of physical satisfaction. Man does not live by

[28]

bread alone. He is driven by the desire "for power, or for love, or for destruction, he risks his life for religious, for political, for humanistic ideals, and these strivings are what constitute and characterize the peculiarity of human life." [1] In contrast to the animal, man knows that he lives, and this knowledge makes him restless and anxious about his life. He exists, and, unlike everything else, he knows that he exists. He is a part of nature and his physical needs must be satisfied, but he also transcends nature; he is self-conscious, and so he ponders about the meaning of his life. Because he is not only finite but also infinite, he is always discontented and inquisitive, concerned about his destiny.

Fromm's view of the transcendent or infinite element of human nature must not be misconstrued. His interpretation is not to be equated with, say, the position held by Reinhold Niebuhr. Niebuhr identified the infinite dimension of man with the Biblical *imago Dei*—that is, with the idea that man is a creature of God and that only through the Creator can human life be fulfilled.[2] This is exactly what Fromm does not want to assert. Fromm's view is more in keeping with that of Ludwig Feuerbach. The philosopher Feuerbach believed that man is radically different from the brute: "Man thinks—that is, he converses with himself." "Man is himself at once I and thou. . . ." And it is precisely for this reason that both individual man and the species of man can become the object of human thought. And man's religion is a phenomenon "identical with self-consciousness—with the consciousness which man has of his nature." Or, what is the same, religion is "consciousness of the infinite." But what does Feuerbach mean by the infinite? "The consciousness of the infinite is nothing else than the conscious-

ness of the infinity of the consciousness; or, in the consciousness of the infinite, the conscious subject has for his object
the infinity of his own nature." [3] Fromm's position parallels
Feuerbach's: infinity is accounted for in human, not divine,
terms.

Man's "freakish" condition, continues Fromm, of being
finite and infinite, part of the animal world and yet tran-
scending it, is the occasion for his relentless struggle for a
meaningful orientation. The superiority that man has gained
through his evolutionary development turns out to be a mixed
blessing. For in his superiority he becomes poignantly aware
of himself and of the powerlessness and limitations of his life,
of the incongruities and disruption of his existence. Other animals know nothing of this predicament. Fromm says, "Man is
the only animal for whom his own existence is a problem
which he has to solve and from which he cannot escape." [4]
His very nature precludes the possibility of an existence of
cold indifference or of complete contentment. The apathy and
harmony of the prehuman stage is lost through the evolutionary process. Or to put the point differently, man "is expelled
from Paradise, and two angels with fiery swords prevent his
return." [5] The human being is the eternal wanderer—Odys-
seus, Oedipus, Abraham, Faust. He must resign himself to the
loss of his natural home and go out and create a new one—
one "which can lift the curse by which he was separated from
nature, from his fellow men, and from himself." [6]

The plight of man can be explained more concretely in
terms of several basic "existential dichotomies." The term "existential dichotomies" signifies certain conflicts and divisions
that are intrinsic to human existence. They do not arise through

[30]

human contriving and therefore cannot be casually brushed aside—as Samson disposed of the lion—as though they were temporary obstacles along the way; they are inexorable, and while they can be parried, they cannot be annulled. One of these dichotomies is "life and death." Death is inevitable; yet it is incompatible with life, it is the opposite of life. And all the knowledge available cannot abrogate the fact that death represents defeat—the end. There is no easy way out of this ill-fated state. Men have tried to mitigate and avoid it through the idea of immortality—the idea that the soul never dies and death is not real—but this is too anemic.

A second dichotomy is this: because of man's short span of life his potentialities are never fully realized. "Man's life, beginning and ending at one accidental point in the evolutionary process of the race, conflicts tragically with the individual's claim for the realization of all of his potentialities." [7] Death is the premature termination of all occasions for growth and creative living. Again, this human plight generates ideologies which serve as compensatory measures. Man is advised, for example, that life will be fulfilled after death, or the line is taken that the real satisfaction of life is gained through devotion to the welfare of the state, the community, or some other group which transcends the individual. But such counsel is not a real answer.

A third dichotomy involves man's frightening awareness that he is alone. Man is a separate and independent being; he exists as a solitary figure; yet, he longs to be related to his fellow men. He is, in fact, one whose well-being depends upon a meaningful relationship with others. Caught in this antinomy man generally tries to resolve it by escaping from his freedom

[31]

—through one of two ways: he submits to somebody or something outside of himself, some authoritarian power, or he tries to dominate somebody or something in this outside world by compelling it to be a part of himself. But, of course, both escapes are disastrous in that they obliterate the individuality and integrity of the self.[8]

In addition to the existential dichotomies, Fromm points out that man is also involved in "historical dichotomies." These dichotomies are the contradictions and paradoxes of life that are not a part of existence as such; they are man-made and, unlike the existential ones, can be annulled. For example, slavery in ancient Greece was an injustice; yet this condition was not ineluctable—through the redistribution of wealth it was wiped out. Again, there is the contemporary conflict involving man's vast technical means and his failure to use them exclusively for peace and the welfare of the people; yet, this conflict is not insoluble—granted sufficient wisdom and courage it can be eliminated. The historical dichotomies are relatively ephemeral and wieldy and do not touch the heart of the matter. It is the existential dichotomies that pull and jolt the center of life and cause man to seek meaning. The existential level is the occasion for religion. *"The necessity to find ever-new solutions for the contradictions in his existence, to find ever-higher forms of unity with nature, his fellow men and himself, is the source of all psychic forces which motivate man, of all his passions, affects and anxieties* [of all religion]." [9]

How then can man's enigmatic existence be illuminated? How can the existential dichotomies be resolved? How can man achieve self-realization? Fromm's answer, as already indicated, is "humanistic ethics." The power to realize true life lies within man himself. By trusting his own intelligence, ingenuity, and goodness, man can both define the nature of excellence and become the incarnation of it. Protagoras was right: "Man is the measure of all things." All purposes and values of man's existence are derived solely from the human dimension. Accordingly, the primary and crucial question is, What is the nature of man? What are the contours of his being, the vital forces of his life? To know man is to know what is good for man. Ethics is concerned with "achieving excellence in performing the art of living." [10] But only after we know what qualities and powers are latent within, what man really is, can we prescribe the norm for the life of excellence. To put it somewhat differently, authentic existence is tantamount to the actualization of the fundamental faculties and propensities of man's being. To truly live is to actualize certain qualities latent within the self. *"Existence and the unfolding of the specific powers of an organism are one and the same. All organisms have an inherent tendency to actualize their specific potentialities. The aim of man's life, therefore, is to be understood as the unfolding of his powers according to the laws of his nature."* [11] Thus, again, the initial and pre-eminent question is, What is man?

Fromm, like the American philosopher John Dewey, regards science as the authentic medium for discovering all truth, including the truth about man. For Dewey, the "new methods of inquiry and reflection [scientific methods] have become for the educated man today the final arbiter of all questions of fact, existence, and intellectual assent." [12] And Fromm agrees: The only aims and ideals which warrant approbation are those which can be reconciled with science. Sociology, anthropology, and, more particularly, psychoanalysis—these are the means through which man and the ideals befitting him can be known. Of course, it must be acknowledged that the sciences can observe, not human nature as such, but only its reactions and manifestations so that the final description of man's nature must be inferred from the empirical observations. Yet it must also be noted that this fact is not peculiar to the scientific study of man but is true of all sciences "which operate with concepts of entities based on, or controlled by, inferences from observed data and not directly observable themselves." [13]

Assuming the unconditional authority of science, Fromm proceeds to delineate his principal thesis. Through the eyes of science, he maintains, man perceives that the desire to live is indigenous to human nature; in fact, it is the most obstinate and decisive thrust of man's entire being. Psychologists refer to it as the "instinct" of self-preservation. Man does not decide whether he wants to live or die—the first principle of his being is to be alive. And from this follows the moral maxim concerning virtue: "Virtue is proportional to the degree of productiveness a person has achieved." [14] Productiveness, of course, must not be equated with the capacity to create a symphony, a novel, or a painting, even though such artistic expressions are evidences of an effective life. Productiveness is, rather, the realization of man's potentialities; it is an attitude, a mode of relatedness, which may be peculiar to every man. Moreover, productiveness is not synonymous with activity. Activity is an expenditure of energy and brings about a change, but it is not necessarily—though, of course, it may be—a humanly edifying enterprise. Activity is productive only insofar as the potentialities characteristic of man are realized.

There are two distinct means through which the productive life becomes a reality: acting and comprehending. "Man *produces things,* and in the process of creation he exercises his powers over matter. Man *comprehends the world,* mentally and emotionally, through love and through reason. His power of reason enables him to penetrate through the surface and to grasp the essence of his object by getting into active relation with it. His power of love enables him to break through the wall which separates him from another person and to comprehend him." [15]

Real love, or "productive love," has certain basic elements, and among them are "care and responsibility." These two ingredients represent the fact that love is "not a passion by which one is overcome" but rather a concern for the growth and development of the other person. Also, love includes the components of "respect and knowledge." "Respect" denotes "the ability to see a person as he is, to be aware of his individuality and uniqueness." And "knowledge"—the prerequisite for respect—means to comprehend, to penetrate "through the surface of things in order to discover their essence, their hidden relationships and deeper meanings, their 'reason.'" [16]

Also, the thinking peculiar to the productive orientation has certain characteristics. First, it is intensely interested in the other person, or phenomenon, not detached from it; in fact, "the more intimate this relation is, the more *fruitful*" the thinking. Yet, in the involvement of reason the integrity of the object of thought is not violated, the object is always respected and viewed as it actually is, as "it exists according to its own nature." Secondly, in productive thinking, the object must be seen in its totality. To observe only part of it inevitably results in a distorted apprehension. Thirdly, productive thinking re-

[35]

quires that one must not only see the object as it is but also see oneself as one is. There must be an awareness "of the particular constellation in which one finds oneself as an observer related to the object of observation." [17]

And what of productive activity? "Productive activity is characterized by the rhythmic change of activity and repose. Productive work, love, and thought are possible only if a person can be, when necessary, quiet and alone with himself. To be able to listen to oneself is a prerequisite for the ability to listen to others; to be at home with oneself is the necessary condition for relating oneself to others." [18]

The productive orientation, as conceived by human intelligence, is the epitome of all goodness. No moral claim supersedes or equals man's obligation to affirm his life, to actualize the attributes peculiar to his nature. Yet, this orientation of excellence does not always obtain. There are other ways of living, quite antithetical to the productive one, which diminish, if not fully destroy, the vitality and life-giving substance of human existence. Fromm lists and describes four such orientations: "receptive," "exploitative," "hoarding," and "marketing."

The "receptive orientation" represents the persons who feel that everything good is derived from sources beyond themselves; they rely upon others rather than upon themselves. They are always ready to receive but are not able to give. If they are religious, they depend not on their own reason but on the edicts of an omniscient being. Since they desperately need the help and loyalty of others—people or a god—they can easily say Yes but find it hard to say No. They cannot bear to be alone and are exceedingly sensitive to the rebuffs of others. They fear to affirm themselves lest the harmony established through their subordination to others be disrupted.

The "exploitative orientation" is also characterized by a belief in the idea that all good is derived from the outside and that one cannot produce anything oneself. The difference is that people who belong to the exploitative type, unlike those who belong to the receptive type, do not expect to receive through the graciousness of others; their method is to grab and steal. The ideas and material possessions which they can swindle from others appear more attractive than the ones they can produce themselves. They thrive on exploiting everyone and everything. Since they are satisfied only with the stolen product, they underrate their own abilities and possessions. An exaggerated expression of the exploitative type is the kleptomaniac, who enjoys stealing what he could well afford to purchase.

The "hoarding orientation" represents the effort to build a protective wall around oneself and to keep as little as possible of one's worldly goods from getting away. To enjoy something or someone, one must possess it. The past is glorified; the memories of yesterday's feelings and experiences are enjoyed nostalgically. These persons say "no" rather than "yes" because they fear intrusion. They hold onto everything they have and their dictum for justice is "Mine is mine and yours is yours."

The "marketing orientation" is identified especially with the modern era. The essence of this orientation is that one must sell himself, as a commodity is sold on the market. Clerks and salesmen, business executives and doctors, lawyers, and artists —all of them have to "sell" their personalities in order to sell their products or services. An individual's success is dependent upon the salability of himself. Do people like his personality? Is he "cheerful," "sound," "aggressive," "reliable," "ambitious"? What is his social background and religious affiliation? According to Fromm: "In the marketing orientation man encounters his own powers as commodities alienated from him. He is not one with them but they are masked from him because what matters is not his self-realization in the process of using them but his success in the process of selling them." His formula is *I am as you desire me.*" [19]

These negative orientations, Fromm declares, must be repudiated. The only orientation that is valid is the productive one, the one identified with humanistic ethics. In upholding this view he claims that he reflects the thoughts of Aristotle, Spinoza, Goethe, Ibsen, Dewey, and other enlightened thinkers who asserted that man is an autonomous being, and that the fulfillment of man's nature as prescribed by human intelligence is the essence of the good life. Fromm's formula for living is, in essence, a recapitulation of the humanist's credo of self-sufficiency, a creed of which he is unabashedly proud.

But he does not yet rest his case. Seemingly, he assumes that the validity and cogency of humanistic ethics become increasingly evident if it is seen in relation to the contrary point of view, this view being "authoritarian ethics" as propagated by the Christian faith. Accordingly, he delineates the latter position, setting forth the major criticism that one of the most baneful facts about authoritarian ethics is that it trusts God and distrusts man; it holds that God is everything, man is nothing. The authoritarian conscience, he contends, damns the very qualities which ought to be extolled: the feeling of strength, independence, and pride. For according to Luther and Calvin, who are, says Fromm, the chief purveyors of this ruinous gospel, nothing is more demonic than the humanistic claim that man is everything. The preposterous and infidel ideal that man can save himself must, the reformers insist, be totally repudiated.

Fromm believes that authoritarian ethics can be characterized by two criteria—one *"formal,"* the other *"material."* In *Man for Himself,* he says:

> Formally, authoritarian ethics denies man's capacity to know what is good or bad; the norm giver is always an authority transcending the individual. Such a system is based not on reason and knowledge but on awe of the authority and on the subject's feeling of weakness and dependence; the surrender of decision making to the authority results from the latter's magic power; its decisions can not and must not be questioned. Materially, or according to content, authoritarian ethics answers the question of what is good or bad primarily in terms of the interests of the authority, not the interest of the subject; it is exploitation, although the subject may derive considerable benefits, psycho or material, from it.[20]

In these two ways authoritarian ethics is completely inimical to humanistic ethics for, according to the latter, all goodness is derived from human existence and only those values merit acclaim which enrich the life of not God but man. "Humanistic ethics is anthropocentric; not, of course, in the sense that man is the center of the universe but in the sense that his value judgments, like all other judgments and even perceptions, are rooted in the peculiarities of his existence and are meaningful only with reference to it; man, indeed, is the 'measure of all things.' The humanistic position is that there is nothing higher and nothing more dignified than human existence." [21]

The essential character of the authoritarian motif, Fromm explains, is represented in the experience of the child who accepts the parent's word as to what is "good" and "bad." The child does not reason a problem out. Indeed, he cannot; he simply adopts the ethical code as issued by his elders. And the adult in his social existence encounters a similar condition. "Good" is that which is approved by society, and "bad" is that which is disapproved. And in view of man's strong predilection to gain the esteem and sanction of his fellow men, particularly of his peers, he readily accepts the code of life prescribed by the social group. Both the child and the adult, caught in the grasping hands of external powers, are too fearfully paralyzed to question the authenticity of the way of life imposed upon them. In this same manner, authoritarian ethics controls from without. It intimidates man into submission to an almighty being, and man's worth is determined by his compliance to the will of this being. God has certain ambitions and He bestows his approval upon all persons who serve His ends. The designs of the Supreme Being must be furthered, not blocked. Analogies are legion. A hunting dog is called "good" because it is useful to its owner. A student is "good" if he obeys the teacher. A child is "good" if he acquiesces to his parents. This is the logic of authoritarianism. But what if God's demands are absurd? Men must obey! "Theirs not to make reply, theirs not to reason why, theirs but to do and die." God will not tolerate any human initiative—particularly free, rational inquiry. In the story of Adam and Eve as told in Genesis, no reason is given as to *why* eating from the tree in the center of the garden was evil; the first man and woman were simply informed in an arbitrary manner that the fruit of a particular tree must not be eaten. And because they were unwilling to prostrate themselves in dutiful obedience, they were upbraided.

Within authoritarian ethics the impelling thrust is the coveted premium of being accepted by God. The pleasure of enjoying this divine approval is acclaimed to be the greatest favor man can desire. And the price for obtaining it is never too exorbitant. Man will immolate his freedom and integrity if only he can gain the security that comes from identification with God. Or, to put the point negatively, the worst calamity which can befall man is to be rejected by God. Punishment, in whatever form it may take, is always better than rejection for this reason: punishment could not occur if God were totally absent, while rejection denotes the tragic isolation from God. The Biblical parable of Cain and Abel suggests something of the agony and misery experienced by those who feel rejected by God. According to the story, the two brothers offered sacrifices, but Abel's gift was accepted while Cain's was rejected. Cain's plight was more than he could bear because God's unwillingness to accept his offering was tantamount to the repudiation of Cain himself. The condition of losing God's favor was the worst fate possible; nothing could be more terrible. Cain was an outcast who had to go it alone, separated from God and his fellow men.

According to the authoritarian scheme, man is in himself of no account. The will of a sovereign master is everything. Authoritarian ethics denies precisely that which humanistic ethics asserts. The latter conceives the good to be the awareness of the right as derived from human experience and thought. It is the reaction, not of ourselves to God, but of "ourselves to ourselves." "It is the voice of our true selves which summons us back to ourselves, to live productively, to develop fully and harmoniously—that is, *to become what we potentially are*." [22] But authoritarian ethics bases everything on the voice of an external, supernatural power. Luther, for example, contends that the real norm and true power of man is derived from a superhuman being before whom man must humble and sacrifice himself. Fromm quotes Luther's statement: ". . . God wants to save us not by our own but by extraneous (*fremde*) justice and wisdom, by a justice that does not come from ourselves and does not originate in ourselves but comes to us from somewhere else. . . . That is, a justice must be taught that comes exclusively from the outside and is entirely alien to ourselves." [23] So the person is bound to the wishes and dictates of an external authority. The ethical behavior ordered by God must be heeded, not because it is good—for, humanly speaking, it may not be good—but simply because it is the divine will. The condition of human virtue is that of walking before the Almighty in trepidation and in unconditional obedience. Also, in *Escape from Freedom,* Fromm notes what Calvin has written in his *Institutes* regarding this matter:

We are not our own; therefore neither our reason nor our will should predominate in our deliberations and actions. We are not our own; therefore, let us not propose it as our end, to seek what may be expedient for us according to the flesh. We are not our own; therefore, let us, as far as possible, forget ourselves and all things that are ours. On the contrary, we are God's; to him, therefore, let us live and die. For, as it is the most devastating pestilence which ruins people if they obey themselves, it is the only haven of salvation not to know or to want anything oneself but to be guided by God who walks before us. [24]

The strictures of the authoritarian conscience against human initiative and self-reliance are most severe, says Fromm. The authoritarians insist that man is man and God is God and that the worst sin conceivable is for man to deny his humanness and to equate himself pretentiously with the Almighty. The sin of Adam and Eve was that they wanted to be like God, and it was precisely because of this inordinate ambition that they were expelled from the Garden of Eden. God and man are infinitely different, and the most telling attestation of this fact is that the Almighty is the source of all will and cannot be subjected to the will of others. God himself creates and is never created; He alone enjoys the privilege of both willing and creating. And in light of this condition human virtue springs from the willingness to be ruled and molded according to the divine design. Human personality is worthless and base and in the name of Almighty God must be destroyed. This idea was, Fromm avers, at the center of Luther's thought. In *Escape from Freedom* he says:

Luther's relationship to God was one of complete submission. In psychological terms his concept of faith means: if you completely submit, if you accept your individual insignificance, then the all-powerful God may be willing to love you and save you. If you get rid of your individual self with all its shortcomings and doubts by utmost self-effacement, you free yourself from the feeling of your own nothingness and can participate in God's glory. Thus while Luther freed people from the authority of the Church, he made them submit to a much more tyrannical authority, that of a God who insisted on complete submission of man and annihilation of the individual self as the essential condition to his salvation. *Luther's "faith" was the conviction of being loved upon the condition of surrender,* a solution which has much in common with the principle of complete submission of the individual to the state and the "leader." [25]

Fromm's exploration and appraisal of "humanistic ethics" and "authoritarian ethics" have already covered a considerable territory, but there remains one area which calls for additional attention: it is the matter of the goodness and evilness of man. Does man's moral fiber warrant and justify his trust in himself? Alas! Fromm laments, the myopic Christian theologians see man as sinful, impotent, and ignominious; thus, their trust in external powers. They scowl at the idea that man could be genuinely virtuous. St. Augustine insisted that "man's nature was corrupt since the fall, that each generation was born with the curse caused by the first man's disobedience, and that only God's grace, transmitted by the Church and her sacraments, could save man." [26] Centuries later Thomas Aquinas challenged the Augustinian thesis by crediting human nature with uprightness, dignity, and power. But the Protestant Reformation ushered in the old pessimism, and man was once more assaulted as a contemptible and depraved being. Fromm quotes Calvin's assertion that not a single "work of a pious man ever existed which, if it were examined before the strict judgment of God, did not prove to be damnable." Also, "it is an ancient and true observation that there is a world of vices concealed in the soul of man." [27] The evil is ingrained so deeply that man himself cannot eradicate it; the only remedy is to deny the self and discard all selfish considerations, and to be solely concerned about pleasing God.

And Luther, says Fromm, is equally derogatory in his appraisal of man. He holds that there is within man an innate evil-

ness which taints all human thought and conduct. Even the
noblest deeds of man are perverted by the inordinate love of
the self. Luther's commentary on the Book of Romans is a clear
expression of his idea of the vile and meritless nature of man.
Fromm cites a statement found at the very beginning of the
commentary: "The essence of this letter [Romans] is: to destroy, to uproot, and to annihilate all wisdom and justice of
the flesh, may it appear—in our eyes and in those of others—
ever so remarkable and sincere. . . . What matters is that
our justice and wisdom which unfold before our eyes are being
destroyed and uprooted from our heart and from our vain
self." [28] Luther's theology is saturated with the idea of the
depravity of man and of his impotence. As evidence of this
fact, Fromm quotes from a pamphlet in which Luther attacked
Erasmus: "Thus the human will is, as it were, a beast between
the two. If God sit thereon, it wills and goes where God will;
as the Psalm saith, 'I was as a beast before thee; nevertheless
I am continually with thee.' (Ps. 73:22,23) If Satan sit thereon,
it wills and goes as Satan will. Nor is it in the power of its own
will to choose, to which rider it will run, nor which it will seek;
but the riders themselves contend, which shall have and hold
it." [29]

Fromm then offers his positive view regarding the issue
of the goodness and evilness of man. The term "good," he explains, is synonymous with constructive living, with the unfolding of the powers latent within man, with the fulfillment of
the emotional, physical, and intellectual capacities of the human personality. To live the life of self-realization is to live
virtuously. On the other hand, "evil" refers to the absence of
the good, to the powers which thwart and block the develop-

ment of the personality. Evil is that which disallows the good. Thus, "good" and "evil" are correlated in that the one is present to the extent that the other is absent. Or, as Fromm explains the matter, "the life-destructive forces in a person occur in an inverse ratio to the life-furthering ones; the stronger the one the weaker the other, and vice versa." [30]

In view of the evidence of both good and evil within man, is it accurate to conclude that man harbors equal potentialities for both of them? Fromm's answer is No. The term "potentiality," it is true, means not only that a condition will exist in the future but that the future existence is already prepared in the present. But now the question arises: Does this mean that the future stage will *necessarily* come into existence because the present stage exists? No, not necessarily. The actualization occurs only if the propitious conditions are present. For example, a seed will become a tree, and will not rot, only if it is properly nourished. Accordingly, the seed really possesses two kinds of potentialities: one is a *"primary potentiality,* which is actualized if the proper conditions are present," i.e., the potentiality for goodness; and the other is a *"secondary potentiality,* which is actualized if conditions are in contrast to existential needs," i.e., the potentiality for evilness.[31] Accordingly, Fromm takes his stand: man is primarily good, and given the right conditions this goodness is realized. Barring some "unnatural" obstruction he will "naturally" be good, for there is no question but that "the normal individual possesses in himself the tendency to develop, to grow, to be productive." [32] In fact, man's disposition toward self-fulfillment and productive living is not simply a moral trait but is characteristic of his entire being. Man has the capacity to walk and move, and the paralysis of

[46]

these powers results in discomfort and illness; women have the power to bear children, and sterility usually brings frustrations; Freud pointed out that the blocking of sexual energy evokes neurotic disturbances. So, by the same logic, man has the capacity to speak and think and love, and if these powers are unexercised man becomes truncated and warped. Man is primarily good.

Erich Fromm's stand regarding religion and the Christian faith is clear. He has espoused religion of the "humanistic ethic" variety as the condition whereby the life of man is properly enhanced and fulfilled. Fromm's god is man himself, his messiah is the scientific method, and his gospel is one of self-reliance. He is unabashedly confident that the only reasonable and befitting religion is one grounded in a faith in man. The Christian faith is inimical to true religion. Its emphasis on the supremacy and goodness of God and on the impotence and vileness of man is offensive and dangerous to humanity. St. Paul, St. Augustine, Luther, Calvin (and among the contemporaries Fromm might have mentioned Barth, Brunner, and Niebuhr)—all of these men patronize a gospel which derogates rather than ennobles human life. In fact, even the father of liberalism, Schleiermacher, whose view is not completely inimical to humanism, is dismissed by Fromm as one who defined religion in terms of the "masochistic experience in general." [33] True religion, Fromm concludes, is that which dispossesses the Christian's superhuman being of its illicit authority and reinstates man with the right to rule himself. For Fromm, Feuerbach was right: "The beginning, middle and end of religion is MAN." [34]

CHAPTER 3 The Christian Faith Without Religion: Dietrich Bonhoeffer

DIETRICH BONHOEFFER *was born in 1906 in Breslau, Germany. His father, whose forebears numbered several parsons, was a distinguished psychiatrist and a professor at Berlin University. His mother was a granddaughter of Karl von Hase, an eminent professor of church history. During Dietrich's childhood his playmates included the children of Adolf von Harnack, a famous theologian, and of Hans Delbrück, a famous historian. Later, as a student at the University of Berlin, he became acquainted with such great teachers as Harnack, Seeberg, and Lietzmann, but more importantly, he came under the influence of the theology of Karl Barth. After his formal training he served as a pastor in Barcelona (1928–1929), studied at Union Theological Seminary, New York City (1930), and then returned to Berlin to teach in the university, where he remained until forbidden to stay longer by the National-Socialist authori-*

ties in 1936. It was during his stint at the university that he also took charge of the German congregations of St. Paul and Syden- ham in London. Later, he was called by the Confessing Church in Germany to return home to lead an emergency seminary in Pomerania for young ministers, at which time he wrote two of his renowned works: THE COST OF DISCIPLESHIP *and* GEMEINSAMES LEBEN. *Thereafter, events occurred that changed the entire direction of his life. Through his brother-in-law, Hans von Dohnanyi, he became identified with the resistance movement and its endeavor to overthrow the Nazi government. His iden- tification with this subversive effort was discovered by the Gestapo, and in April, 1943, Bonhoeffer was arrested and taken to Tegel Prison. Following the unsuccessful plot to kill Hitler on July 20, 1944, and the subsequent discovery by the Gestapo of incriminating information against Bonhoeffer, the German pastor was transferred to the Prinz Albert Strasse Prison, and then later to Buchenwald, Schönberg, and Flossenbürg, in that order. Finally, on Monday, April 9, 1945, Bonhoeffer was taken to the scaffold, where he met his death.*

ACCORDING to the late Dietrich Bonhoeffer, Erich Fromm has been viewing things upside down: when religion and the Christian faith are seen in their *proper* perspective it is the Christian faith and not religion that is singularly crucial and indispensable. The fact is, Bonhoeffer asserts, that religion is not simply a dispensable phenomenon but a part of human ex- istence with which modern man *has already* dispensed. The common assertion that man is naturally religious, a priori reli- gious, is simply not true. The present situation clearly reveals that modern man is more or less removed from the preoccupations and anxieties peculiar to the religious life. Man has "become of age," says Bonhoeffer. The modern scene is not one in which man walks in a cemetery, despairingly and forsakenly crying out, What is the meaning of it all? He has learned to deal with the existential twists and splits of life, including the one generally proclaimed to be the most dreadful—the fact of death. Man confidently holds his destiny in his own hands; neither distraught by the so-called estrangements nor confounded by the supposed dichotomies, he appears to be self-contained. This is the religionless man of the modern era. And the prophets and apologists of the Christian faith must take cognizance of this fact, Bonhoeffer warns. It is erroneous to view Christianity as a concomitant of religion and as a phenomenon which acquires intelligibility and approbation through its juxtaposition to the concerns of religion. The Christian faith has its own *raison d'être* and is fully explicable and constraining apart from any religious involvements. The Christian faith, according to traditional theology, is man's response to God through Christ, the gospel supremely true and good. This faith, Bonhoeffer insists, must be decoded so that twentieth-century man can read it apart from all religion.

Before I proceed to elaborate on Bonhoeffer's thesis, a brief discussion of the general theological and philosophical worlds within which he lived and to which he responded will, perhaps, help to shed light upon his fresh approach to the Christian faith. Bonhoeffer was primarily concerned with this question: How is Christ to be reclaimed for a world which has come of age? It was his belief that modern times constitute a peculiar challenge to Christianity. He was convinced that, in at least one respect, the traditional apology for the Christian faith is no longer valid. These were ideas which Bonhoeffer held, and, if we are to grasp something of their import, they must not be viewed apart from two historical developments: Christianity and the Enlightenment.

Bonhoeffer's life and thought are grounded in the Christian faith—to be more exact, they are grounded in the Christian faith as interpreted within the Barth-Kierkegaard-Luther-Augustine-Paul tradition. In other words, the general tenor of his theology is in keeping with the more traditional rendition of the Christian faith. The traditional theologians believed that faith begins with the acceptance of the fact of God. God is acknowledged to be a personal being who created man and the world and is infinitely concerned about His creation. God is a living god who made all things; God is absolutely free, absolutely transcendent, and absolutely loving. There is no place in Bonhoeffer's theology for the notion that God is an impersonal reality who caused the world to come into existence but is now removed from the affairs of the world, coolly sitting by, watching as the universe runs according to its inherent mechanical and rational laws. No! God is an active god and His ways are infinitely different from the ways of man. What God is and what God does cannot be contained in any intellectual system or human category; that which is Godly defies all comprehension by the finite mind. Only by knowing God does one know the truth, and only by acknowledging His Lordship does one have righteousness. Everything proceeds from God. "Herein is love, not that we loved God, but that he loves us, and sent his Son to be the propitiation for our sins." "We love him because he first loved us." All things are dependent upon

God, including the extent to which man can know Him and the degree to which man's life can be related to Him. In summary, Bonhoeffer stands upon the traditional affirmation that God is the Creator of the world and in His sovereign will is working out His righteousness in history; all men depend upon Him, for He is both their Creator and their Redeemer.

Man, according to the theological claims, must be viewed as a sinful creature, one who has fallen from his original state of goodness. When the world began, God created Adam in His own image, and God saw that the creation of man was good. But the serpent induced Adam to rebel against God, to try to do something to become like the Almighty. In this act of defiance of God, man sinned against Him, and the "image" was defaced. What happened then? "Since that day," says Bonhoeffer, "the sons of Adams in their pride have striven to recover the divine image by their own efforts. But the more they try, and the more apparent their success, the more alienated from God they become. Their misshapen form, modelled after the god they have invented for themselves, grows more and more like the image of Satan, though they are unaware of it. The Divine image, which God in His grace had given to man, is lost forever on this earth." [1]

Jesus Christ, it has been traditionally claimed, is God's revelation of Himself to man. In Christ, God entered history, coming to man in the form of a servant. In the acts of Christ, in his life and death, the "image of God has been recreated on earth." Christ is not the teacher of mankind, the great prophet, the example of religious and moral life for all time; He is the incarnation of God in the world. In Christ, God comes to the world of sin and death, and, like a servant, He takes upon

Himself the sins and sorrows of mankind. "He was wounded for our transgressions, He was bruised for our iniquities." "Surely He hath borne our griefs, and carried our sorrows." In both life and death Jesus received sinners and took them to Himself. It is Christ "who meekly bears God's wrath and judgment against sinners, and obeys His will with unswerving devotion in suffering and death, the Man born to poverty, the friend of publicans and sinners, the Man of sorrows, rejected of man and forsaken of God. Here is God made man, here is man in the new image of God." [2]

Faith, according to the more orthodox reasoning, is man's response to God through Christ, and, in this response of faith through grace, it is said, lies man's justification. Faith is nothing else than receiving the Word which was made known in Christ. The man of faith puts his life into the hands of God; the man of faith knows that his salvation and his justification cannot be found within himself but that they come only through Jesus Christ. He knows that his entire life is dependent upon the power and love of God. Good works and sound doctrines will not deliver him from his destitution and death. Only the Word, only the image, as given by Jesus Christ can save him. Bonhoeffer recalls the expression of the reformers: the righteousness of man is an "alien righteousness," a righteousness that comes from outside of man. Man is helpless to effect his own spiritual restitution. "The Christian," asserts Bonhoeffer, "no longer lives of himself, by his own claims and his own justification, but by God's claims and God's justification. He lives wholly by God's Word pronounced upon him, whether that Word declares him guilty or innocent." [3]

The account of the traditional Christian affirmations need

not be continued; the general line of reasoning of this theology is evident in sufficient measure to reveal its peculiar theological nature. The only additional word—and a very important one, for it was the one that Bonhoeffer later disclaimed—about this theological perspective that is required is this: its underlying supposition is that Christianity is the ultimate answer to the human question, that it delivers man from the pale of destitution and redeems man from the guilt of sin. Through faith, it is assumed, man receives the courage and the hope which his soul desperately longs for. In other words, permeating this interpretation of Christianity was the belief that man is a frail, finite, ignorant, and sinful creature and that he is forever dissatisfied with his life and anxious about his salvation. The gospel, it is believed, is proclaimed with the idea that it is the word of salvation providing strength and compassion to the forlorn creature, man, who is wringing his hands and is torn apart inwardly because of the dark state of his soul. The gospel delivers man from the "miry clay." Stated somewhat differently, it is taken for granted that unless the individual knows and acknowledges his wretchedness he will not be able to respond meaningfully to the message of the gospel. For how could one be lifted up unless one were first spiritually depressed? Thus the faith is meaningful only as one first confesses his depravity and is involved in existential despair.

In addition to Christian theology, there was a second great tradition that had a definite and peculiar influence upon Bonhoeffer's thought: the humanistic movement of the seventeenth and eighteenth centuries. As Bonhoeffer views the panorama of history, he concludes that the spirit of this particular period of history represents man's ascendancy to a "new age," an age characterized by man's realization of his own power and independence. The apologists for this humanistic faith are, of course, legion. But, according to Bonhoeffer's judgment, a few persons have contributed most significantly to the advent of the "new age." In religion, Lord Herbert of Cherbury takes the lead in the effort to read the Christian faith through the eyes of modern rationalism. The English philosopher insists that the basis for all religious knowledge is reason. He attacks traditional Christian ideas, arguing that man must not subject himself to a blind faith or assent to antiquated doctrines, particularly the old one about the depravity of man. It is his contention that man is essentially good and that the human mind is endowed with the capacity to gain knowledge, including religious knowledge. The ability to reason is what distinguishes man from the animal, and it is by the human intellect that man attains his knowledge of God. Lord Herbert of Cherbury, in his endeavor to lead men away from the traditional interpretation of Christianity, points the way toward deism.

In ethics, Michel de Montaigne, a forerunner of Voltaire, concludes that the Christian ethic is untenable. There are no absolutes and there is no final authority, says Montaigne. Having read widely and examined human existence closely, he is convinced that life assuredly does not offer ultimate moral goals. Even the senses, he argues, cannot be relied upon to provide truth. Sense perception is, after all, relative, and, although man is supposedly distinguished from the animal because of his capacity to understand and feel, it may well be that these capacities are not the exclusive properties of Homo sapiens. And in the realm of reason, says Montaigne, the same kind of uncertainty prevails. Reason is deluding; it projects order, stability, and uniformity into the world of nature, which is, in reality, constantly in flux and without any real unity. Nothing in life is permanent, so one must perforce conclude that there are no eternal moral and religious truths. Montaigne flatly rejects the idea that the ultimate truth has been transmitted from God to man through the revelation of the Biblical faith. Every kind of authority which makes the pretentious assertion of being endowed with the power to apprehend or comprehend the final nature of things must be repudiated.

In politics, Machiavelli emancipated the political ruler from the tutelage of morality. The goal of the ruler, says Machiavelli, is to achieve glory, and, in order to achieve this end, he is at liberty to employ whatever means he deems necessary. Coming closer to the Biblical idea of "original sin" than did many of the enlightened thinkers, Machiavelli believes that the decisions and actions of man are governed by his self-interest. Moreover, he regards man as irrational, easily swayed by emotional appeals, and, therefore, responsive to even the crudest forms of persuasion. Aware of these limitations of man, the skillful ruler does not recoil from the use of force or from whatever means are necessary for the successful manipulation of his subjects. Of course, in the process of wielding his power over his subjects, the leader ought always to cover his actions with the mantles of legality and the sanctions of religion so that he appears to be morally upright. And, in fact, it is expedient that he appear as moral as possible—people will think that he is noble and will praise and trust him more. But, generally speaking, the primary requisite for true leadership is that the leader's mind be "capable of turning in whatever direction the winds of Fortune and the variations of affairs require." For

Machiavelli, political affairs are naturally divorced from all ethical values; political ideas and programs ought to reflect the thought of an ingenious and dexterous human mind, not the will of a just and loving almighty god.

And in philosophy, the renowned rationalist, Descartes, seeks to provide an account of the world without recourse to the Christian God. According to Descartes, God has nothing to do with the functioning of the world, since it operates according to its own mechanistic laws. The material substances of the physical world, Descartes explains, having no locomotive power of their own, are propelled into action by external causes, by a chain of cause-and-effect relationships. And the same explanation holds true for the cosmos. The primary matter of the cosmos, says Descartes, was brought into action by God, and, later, this substance was divided and redivided until it took its present form. God was a part of this process in that He provided the initial push, but, having fulfilled His assignment, He has withdrawn, leaving the world to operate according to its inherent laws. Other than as a first cause, the world has no need for God. Reason and science are perfectly capable of explaining and giving meaning to both terrestrial and celestial realms of life.

In summary, the Enlightenment of the seventeenth and eighteenth centuries, when man staked everything upon man himself, was, it can be said, a time in which the Greek story of Prometheus was re-enacted upon the stage of life: the authority of the god was defied. Prometheus, in Aeschylus's drama, in stealing the fire from heaven, bequeathed to man the power which was previously reserved exclusively for the gods. With this shift of authority from heaven to earth, the gods to whom men formerly looked for wisdom and assurance become obsolete. All superhuman deities became expendable. Modern man, imbued with the Promethean spirit, is presently at work planning his life, confident that he is both sufficiently wise and duly righteous to manipulate the processes of nature and of history so that the destiny of mankind will be forever safe and secure. He seems to be indubitably certain that he has the power to eradicate all maladies of life and to conceive of ideals and to design programs that will guarantee peace and happiness for all mankind.

Christianity and the Enlightenment, then, are the two historical streams of thought which, according to Bonhoeffer, the Christian theologian must take seriously if his exposition of the Christian faith is to gain man's approbation. And it was within these two traditions that Bonhoeffer himself sought to delineate the nature of the gospel. It was at the end of his life, while he was waiting for his death in one of Germany's concentration camps, that he became acutely aware of the bearing that the reasoning of the Enlightenment had upon the Christian faith. The question hit him with a disquieting impact: How can one become a Christian and still not disassociate himself from the modern world? Are not these two ways of life mutually exclusive? On the one hand, Christianity proclaims a gospel of love and hope for all who are poor and destitute; Christ came not to save the righteous but to bring the sinners to repentance. The idea that the Christian faith deals primarily with the man who is spiritually distressed was a generally accepted fact. The word of God, it was asserted, brings comfort to the suffering, hope to the destitute, and forgiveness to the transgressor. In other words, the gospel touches the life of man at the point of man's religious concern, his despair over his impotence, and his anxiety about his salvation. On the other hand, the humanistic tradition of the Enlightenment said, in effect, that man is self-sufficient, that he does not need God; man has outgrown the idea that human life is dependent upon a transcendent, personal being. By virtue of his enlightenment and his self-confidence, man is neither overcome by a sense of helplessness, nor anxious about his salvation. In essence, man has been liberated from religion and all its existential concerns.

It was the conflict of these two traditions that caused Bonhoeffer to raise the question: How is Christ to be reclaimed for a world which has come of age? Shall Christianity proclaim its gospel without regard to the Prometheanism of modern man? Or is there a way whereby one can take seriously the free and autonomous spirit of man and still proclaim the gospel in its pristine purity? Bonhoeffer, convinced that the latter possibility is the only real alternative for Christianity, set forth in sketchy form the idea of a "religionless Christianity."

At the outset, said Bonhoeffer in delineating his "religionless Christianity," it is necessary that preachers and apologists of the Christian faith acknowledge the fact that modern man has learned to live without religion. And in saying this, Bonhoeffer was not unaware that he was departing from his former position. During most of his theological career, Bonhoeffer had, in keeping with the traditional idea, assumed that man is a religious being, and that Christianity is meaningful only as it is related to man's religious consciousness. It was not, as mentioned above, until the end of his life that he first recorded this new perspective of the Christian faith. It must not be forgotten that this later point of view is quite different from the one which is expressed in his earlier theological writings.

While incarcerated in Berlin's Tegel Prison from April 5, 1943, to October 8, 1944—because of his "subversive" efforts in Germany, including his collusion with the unsuccessful plot to kill Hitler on July 20, 1944—Bonhoeffer corresponded with his family and several friends. It is in these letters that he first records his idea of the religionlessness of Christianity. His account is, unfortunately, rather fragmentary; nevertheless, the general contour of his thought is apparent. "We are proceeding," he wrote in one of his letters, "toward a time of no religion at all: men as they are now simply cannot be religious any more. Even those who honestly describe themselves as 'religious' do not in the least act up to it, and so when they say 'religious' they evidently mean something quite different." Religion, which was supposed to be an inherent quality of man, is in fact nothing more than "an historical and temporary form of human self-expression." [4] Man has "come of age." He is self-sufficient and unashamedly confident that he can find life and knowledge without recourse to God.

Yet, says Bonhoeffer, much of Christianity has been oblivious to these proclamations of human freedom, and, contrary to the assertion that man need not be preoccupied about God and salvation, within Christian circles the assumption persists that man is existentially anxious and that it is in the midst of this anxiety that God speaks to man; thus it is that God is conceived to be a "stopgap," who completes the humanly incomplete and resolves the humanly irresolvable. The advocates of the gospel still declare that human beings simply cannot live apart from the tutelage of God, and they say that even though it may be true that "there has been surrender on all secular problems, there still remain the so-called ultimate questions—death, guilt—on which only 'God' can furnish an answer, and which are the reasons why God and the Church and the pastor are needed." [5] And so the propagators of the faith, in their efforts to spread the good news, advise that we must take the righteous and enlightened man by the throat and shake him into a state of helplessness and despair in order that he may heed God's word.

And, among the secularists, Bonhoeffer explains, are those who follow this same method: There are the "existentialist philosophers and the psychotherapists, who demonstrate to secure, contented, happy mankind that it is really unhappy and desperate, and merely unwilling to realize that it is in severe straits it knows nothing at all about, from which only they can rescue it. Wherever there is health, strength, security, simplicity, they spy luscious fruit to gnaw at or to lay their pernicious eggs in. They make it their object first of all to drive men to inward despair, and then it is all theirs. That is secularized methodism." [6]

But all the polemic predicated on sin and despair is of no avail, Bonhoeffer contends. For who is concerned about sin and despair? "A small number of intellectuals, of degenerates, of people who regard themselves as the most important thing in the world and hence like looking after themselves. The ordinary man who spends his everyday life at work, and with his family, and of course with all kinds of hobbies and other interests too, is not affected. He has neither time nor inclination for thinking about his intellectual despair and regarding his modest share of happiness as a trial, a trouble or a disaster." [7] Moreover, and more fundamentally, the religious scheme is, by its very nature, self-defeating. It presupposes that helplessness is an eradicable mark of human nature and that man will of necessity entreat God for help. But, retorts Bonhoeffer, this is not true. Science and human acumen have more and more edged God out of life, but—and this is all-important—instead of grasping for God, man has become increasingly self-reliant, learning that he can get along very well without God. He simply does not need God. Strangely enough, Bonhoeffer is at this point arguing beside Friedrich Nietzsche. The famous (or infamous) German philosopher announced, through Zarathustra, that "God is dead"—that is, that the Christian God is dead. And, amazingly enough, Nietzsche says, the Christians themselves have killed Him. The killing of God came about because the Christians conceived God to be a supernatural completion of the natural incompleteness, an attitude which actually meant that God's existence was dependent upon the ignorance of man. But now, for the enlightened mind, there is no longer a place in the scheme of things for such a god; in the eyes of the scientific and learned person this god is dead. For they do not need a god to fill in the gaps. And, thus, a Christianity predicated on human impotence is fatal. "Christianity," said Nietzsche, "arose for the purpose of lightening the heart; but now it must first make heavy the heart in order to lighten it. Consequently it will perish." [8]

In view of man's idea of the irreligious nature of man, Bonhoeffer cites the error in the thought of three of Protestantism's inveterate theologians: Karl Barth, Paul Tillich, and Rudolf Bultmann. Karl Barth was the first theologian to criticize religion. He maintained (as we shall see later) that the Christian faith is the negation of all religion. He realized the mistake of all the religionists, particularly the liberal theologians, who have as their objective "the clearing of a space for religion in the world or against the world."[9] But, says Bonhoeffer, Barth did not pursue his reasoning to its logical conclusion. The question he should have answered but did not answer is, How can Christ become the Lord even of those with no religion? Therein lies Barth's limitation. He deserts the world and makes it depend upon itself, left to its own devices. Thus, what has happened, Bonhoeffer charges, is that Barth has adopted a "positivism of revelation." In effect, he has declared that man must either accept or reject the entire Biblical account —Virgin Birth, Trinity, and all. Man must either "take it or leave it." But the question remains, What difference could such a mandate make to the religionless working man or to any other man for that matter?[10]

Paul Tillich, too, has tried to interpret the world according to a religious presupposition. All men are, says the Harvard University professor, "ultimately concerned" about their existence—i.e., they are religious. They are anxious, aware that nonbeing is a part of their being. They experience the anxiety of fate and death, of emptiness and meaninglessness, of guilt and condemnation; and these anxieties are the flesh and bones of man's "ultimate concern." Sometimes, of course, "preliminary concerns" are substituted for "ultimate concerns"; nevertheless, even in this idolatrous condition, the fact remains that man is infinitely concerned about his being. Tillich's interpretation is a courageous gesture, Bonhoeffer concedes, but the world could not accept it and so "felt entirely *mis*understood, and rejected the imputation."[11] Moreover, Tillich's suggestion that, many times, men worship idols is nothing more than a "bit of moralizing." "The truth is," says Bonhoeffer, "we've given up worshipping everything, even idols. In fact, we are absolute nihilists."[12]

In his famous essay, "New Testament and Mythology," Rudolf Bultmann announced that the thought of the modern world is molded by science and that if the Christian faith is to be meaningful to our contemporaries it must be demythologized—i.e., the kerygma must be stripped from its mythical framework. Christian preaching cannot expect modern man to accept the mythical view of Biblical times. And a plea for such acceptance is senseless "because there is nothing specifically Christian in the mythical view of the world as such." It is only "the cosmology of a pre-scientific age." Also, man *could not* accept it, "because no man can adopt a view of the world by his own volition—it is already determined for him by his place in history." [13] Bultmann's purpose was to take the world for what it is. Bonhoeffer commends him for his intention but thinks that he, too, failed to go far enough: he failed to interpret the concepts of the New Testament "in such a way as not to make religion a pre-condition of faith." [14] While he discarded the old mythology, he retained religion. His theology is shot through with the religious presupposition that man is concerned about "his own real being" and that human *"sin is the point of contact"* for the word of grace.[15]

These eminent theologians overlook the real issue. They do not see that modern man is simply not as dependent and desperate as they conceive him to be, and that it is both pointless and ignoble to attack the world because it is without religion. An attack would be pointless, because it would be an "attempt to put a grown-up man back into adolescence," and it would be ignoble in that it would attempt "to exploit the weakness of man for purposes alien to him and not freely subscribed to by him." [16] Religion is dead, and perhaps man is the better for it. For the God of the "religious" person is not taken seriously; indeed, calling upon His name is not infrequently sheer mockery. Adding an autobiographical note to his general point of view, Bonhoeffer explains in *Prisoner for God:*

. . . Christian instinct frequently draws me more to the religionless than to the religious, by which I mean not with any intention of evangelizing them but rather, I might almost say, in "brotherhood." While I often shrink with religious people from speaking of God by name—because that Name somehow seems to me here not to ring true, and I strike myself as rather dishonest (it is especially bad when others start talking in religious jargon: then I dry up completely and feel somehow oppressed and ill at ease)—with people who have no religion I am able on occasion to speak of God quite openly and as it were naturally. Religious people speak of God when human perception is (often from laziness) at an end, or human resources fail: it is really always the *Deus ex machina* they call to their aid, either for the so-called solving of insoluble problems or as support in human failure—always, that is to say, helping out human weakness or on the borders of human existence. Of necessity, that can only go on until men can, by their own strength, push those borders a little further, so that God becomes superfluous as a *Deus ex machina.* I have come to be doubtful even about talking of "borders of human existence." Is even death to-day, since men are scarcely afraid of it any more, and sin, which they scarcely understand any more, still a genuine borderline? It always seems to me that in talking thus we are only seeking frantically to make room for God.[17]

But not only is a religious Christianity pointless and ignoble; it is also "un-Christian." But, of course, the Church has not recognized this fact. Generally speaking, Christ is represented as the answer to the human cry—emanating from man's religious concern—How can I be saved? Bonhoeffer, though fearful of sounding "pretty monstrous," insists that Christianity's pre-eminent concern is not to "save souls." And to presume that Biblical faith rankles the human soul into a condition of despair and then proceeds to redeem it—to presume this is to misread the Bible. Jesus did not first convict men of sin and then forgive them. It is true that many of them were sinners, but He did not proceed first to make them aware of their evil state. And it is no less true that while Jesus was concerned about the prostitutes, publicans, and outcasts, He was also interested in the spiritually hale and morally hearty. Clearly, Jesus did not set the stage for conversion by reminding men of their sick and weak plight; on the contrary, to the sick He gave health and to the weak He bestowed power. Christ took men for what they were. "The shepherds, like the wise men from the east, stand at the crib, not as converted sinners, but because they were drawn to the crib by the star just as they were. The centurion of Capernaum (who does not make any confession of sin) is held up by Jesus as a model of faith (cf. Jairus). Jesus loves the rich young man. The eunuch (Acts 8), Cornelius (Acts 10) are anything but 'existences over the abyss.' Nathanael is an Israelite without guile (John 1:47)." [18] The distinctive note of the New Testament is not that it saves men from destitution. Bonhoeffer relates that at one time he learned of a French pastor who expressed his desire to become a saint. At the time he was impressed at the parson's seemingly noble ambition. But, later, he saw this incident in a different light—that is, he came to believe that even the desire to become a saint is un-Christian. "One must abandon every attempt to make something of oneself, whether it be a saint, a converted sinner, a churchman (the priestly type, so-called!), a righteous man or an unrighteous one, a sick man or a healthy one." [19]

The idea that Christianity is not a religion of "salvation" is by no means new, says Bonhoeffer; this was a view which was held by Luther. The fragmentary nature of Bonhoeffer's writing at this point is unfortunate since a delineation of the affinity of his "religionless Christianity" to Luther's "justification by faith" would have been very illuminating. As it is, Bonhoeffer simply alludes to Luther, therein inviting us to set it forth more fully. How can the two ideas be brought together? In a provocative book, *The Renewal of Man: A Twentieth Century Essay on Justification by Faith*, Alexander Miller asserts that Luther's *sola gratia, sola fide* was an expression of the irrelevance of religion to the Christian faith. According to the reformer, Miller explains, the Christian is not one who is preoccupied with his spiritual status and valiantly (or humbly, for that matter) set on moving toward a more meritorious rank. Actually, the Christian is one who is indifferent to such a concern. He believes that there are more important matters than the preoccupation with one's soul for the sake of spiritual deliverance. As Miller paraphrases Luther: "It is no longer a question of achieving *my* perfection, or winning *my* salvation, or attaining to *my summum bonum*, for all these are goods for me, and it is this very concern about what is good for me that I am invited to put away." [20] What Luther really does, says Professor Miller, is restate the question of salvation: it is not, How can I be saved? but rather, How can I not be concerned about it? The very concern about salvation, peculiar to religion, precludes the possibility of an authentic life. The pious and the moralistic seek to gain righteousness, but the Christian is not interested in achieving any niche for himself, even that of righteousness. The heart of Luther's "justification by faith" is that man's salvation is really

[68]

an evidence of unbelief. Any form of religious anxiety including piety and moralism is blasphemy; it is evil for man to seek advantage or salvation. The Christian faith ends all religion. "The *sola gratia, sola fide* at which Luther arrives," writes Miller, "is not a solution to the religious question: it is the establishment of a new stance in which the religious question is set aside as irrelevant and impossible of answer in religious terms. What Luther finds in the Gospel is that, not only is the religious question posed with such rigor that it becomes humanly and finally unanswerable, but it becomes finally and forever irrelevant." [21]

But Bonhoeffer's idea that the Biblical message demands a nonreligious interpretation can be viewed from still another vantage point—i.e., his Christology: "What is the nature of Christ?" and, "How can we reclaim for Christ a world which has come of age?"

Christ is the basis for faith. Everything takes on meaning in terms of the revelation of God in Jesus Christ; all that man can expect from God is to be found in Jesus Christ. Christ is *absolutely* crucial. "We think that life has a meaning for us so long as such and such a person still lives. But the truth is that if this earth was good enough for the Man Jesus Christ, if a man like him really lived in it, then, and only then, has life a meaning for us. If Jesus had not lived, then our life, in spite of all the other people we know and honour and love, would be without meaning." [22] Christ is the Lord of man. Only the man who belongs to Christ becomes a true man. The only life worth living is the one which shares in the incarnation, crucifixion, and resurrection of Jesus Christ. In Christ alone is the certainty of faith. He is the basis for faith—i.e., He does not stand as *one* reason beside other reasons and therefore not in Himself supreme, but as if, if one is to be Christian, He must also be believed. He stands alone, and faith means partaking in His existence.

The pre-eminent place of Christology in Bonhoeffer's thought was by no means an innovation, peculiar to the theological slant that emerged during his last days in prison. This was a conviction of long and vigorous standing. Whatever other changes may have occurred in his theology, his Christology never wavered. The centrality of Christ expressed in *Prisoner for God* simply echoes what is found, for example, in his *Ethics*. This work earlier depicts Christ as the revelation of God, the Ultimate Reality, and the apprehension of Ultimate Reality "is the crucial turning-point in the apprehension of reality as a whole." Any effort to understand both the goodness of man and the world must begin with an inquiry about God. For without Him the goodness of men or the goodness of the world have no meaning. "But God as the ultimate reality is no other than He who shows forth, manifests and reveals Himself, that is to say, God in Jesus Christ, and from this it follows that the question of good can find its answer only in Christ." [23]

Ecce homo—Behold the man! He is the Reconciler. In him, through the perfect love of God, the world was reconciled with God. It is not by the idea of love nor by programs of conscience, or duty, or responsibility, or virtue—not by these was the world reconciled, but by the *living* love of God in Jesus Christ. "The figure of the Reconciler, of the God-Man Jesus Christ, comes between God and the world and fills the centre of all history. In this figure the secret of the world is laid bare, and in this figure there is revealed the secret of God." [24] This act of God in Christ is startling and passes all comprehension. God has taken upon Himself the condition of the world. The world is reconciled with God so that God and the world are not two realities but one. God loves the world—not the ideal world, but the real world; He loves man—not the ideal man, but the real man. The very man and world which men "shrink back from with pain and hostility" is the ground for God's unfathomable love, and God unites himself utterly with it.[25]

Ecce homo! In Jesus Christ, God becomes real man, and He desires that we should be real men. In the birth of Christ, God took on manhood in the flesh. He enters into the life of man as man. In this manner He can never be vulnerable to the assertion that His love is ambiguous or not genuine. While we are labeling people ungodly or pious, good or wicked, noble or mean, God makes no distinction; He simply loves the real man. God takes upon himself the character and suffering of man. "Jesus Christ is not the transfiguration of sublime humanity. He is the 'yes' which God addresses to the real man. Not the dispassionate 'yes' of the judge, but the merciful 'yes' of Him who has compassion. In this 'yes' there is comprised the whole life and the whole hope of the world." [26] God through Jesus Christ comes to man and suffers with man. It is this suffering in love which is the good news of the gospel. God comes, and He himself suffers to end the fate of all mankind. Christ, the reality of God, entered into the reality of the world so that whatever happens to God happens to man. God goes with man the whole way. The way of God is the way of suffering—the Cross of Christ.

How then is Christ, the Christ of the suffering God, to be reclaimed for a world which has come of age? Only by bringing together the two realities of Christ and the world. And how shall this be done? It was on this point that Bonhoeffer made a theological about-face. During his pre-prison days he had endorsed the religionist's declaration that man's extremity is God's opportunity and that the humanly unsolvable, unbearable, and unredeemable are God's happy hunting ground. Bonhoeffer had taken the line that the judgment of the Almighty rests upon all men so that all human efforts—religion, ethics, metaphysical knowledge—drip with sin and are of no avail, but that, paradoxically, it is precisely this weak and sinful condition that is the occasion of man's salvation. He believed that the way to find God is through weakness and despair. "There where man himself no longer sees, God sees, and God alone works, in judgment and in grace. There, at the very limits of man, stands God, and when man can do nothing more, then God does all." [27] Desolation and helplessness help to prepare the way for Christ, for "it is precisely to the depths of downfall, of guilt and of misery, that God stoops down in Jesus Christ; that precisely the dispossessed, the humiliated and the exploited, are especially near to the justice and mercy of God; that it is to the undisciplined that Jesus Christ offers His help and His strength; and that the truth is ready to set upon firm ground those who stray and despair." [28]

Then later, while he was in prison, Bonhoeffer altered his point of view. He now believed that bringing faith and religion into an intrinsic relationship with each other does not make Christ the Lord of the world; such a relationship only relegates Christ to the periphery to be employed in times of human exigency. The reclaiming of Christ for the world calls for a perspective in which the elements of integrity and realism are coupled with a sound Christology. Nothing else will do. Thus, reclaiming Christ means, among other things, that one does not gloss over the ungodliness of the world by covering it with a veneer of religion or by frantically trying to transfigure it. The world is accepted in its independent and self-sufficient ways, and, whether in morals, politics, science, religion, or philosophy, God can be dispensed with as a working hypothesis. The Bible itself demands "ultimate honesty" (Matt. 18:3). "And the only way to be honest is to recognize that we have to live in the world *etsi deus non daretur*. And this is just what we do see—before God!" [29] To see the world as godless is to see it as it actually is.

Moreover, reclaiming Christ—and this is at the heart of Bonhoeffer's thought—means that God is found in the center of life. God truly becomes Lord of the world not by catching man as he teeters on the abyss but by meeting him in the *midst* of the world. One must "speak of God," Bonhoeffer writes, "not on the borders of life but as its centre, not in weakness but in strength, not, therefore, in man's suffering and death but in his life and prosperity. On the borders it seems to me better to hold our peace and leave the problem unsolved." [30] God is not to be consigned to "some last secret place," the "boundary situation," as if one must extend the boundaries of life to rescue God from annihilation. The logic of this method is self-destructive, for the frontiers of life are constantly being pushed back so that eventually God would be completely unnecessary as a stopgap. God is at the hub of existence, not at its rim. He is found in health, vigor, activity, and life and not simply in sin, pain, desolation, and death.

According to the Old and New Testaments, says Bonhoeffer, the transcendent, authentic life is the worldly life. Both Testaments forbid man to escape to the eternal by sending him back into the world. The Old Testament is, of course, the story of a redeemed community; but, it must be remembered, "Israel is redeemed out of Egypt in order to live before God on earth." [31] And in the New Testament Christ himself must drink the earthly cup to the lees. Also, the Resurrection is not the answer to the problem of death; it is the transcendence of God, the beyond of God in the midst of our life. To grant that the Christian faith provides release from the cares and burdens of life is to confuse real faith with the "myths of salvation." The salvation myths negate history and are preoccupied with the eternity after death. They seek liberation from this worldly turmoil through ascension to a blissful state beyond the grave, or some other release. But such a clamoring for deliverance is foreign to the way of Christ. Christ takes hold at the center of life, and the Church of Christ "stands not where human powers give out, but in the centre of the village." [32] Jesus calls men, not to a new religion, but to life. The Christian is concerned about this world. "What is above the world is, in the Gospel, intended to exist *for* this world" —to exist "in the Biblical sense of the creation and of the incarnation, crucifixion, and resurrection of Jesus Christ." [33]

In fact, the Christian ought to be a part of the world for the very reason that it is godless. In order that he might reform it? No, this is not the point. It is rather because in its godlessness the world is actually "nearer to God than ever before." [34] Through this world the God before whom we live is teaching us that we can get along without Him, that we do not need Him as a working hypothesis. That is to say, God is weak and powerless in the world. He is a god of suffering. He is not to be used as a *deus ex machina*, as an answer to the religious man's distress. He allows himself to be edged out of the world and to die on a cross. In doing so He teaches us something of the *true* God: not of a god who in his omnipotence helps us solve our problems, who conquers power and space in the world, but of a god who comes in weakness and suffering. In leaving the world godless, God thereby comes to the world. Man's inability to use Him and manipulate Him reveals the God who is beyond all human solicitations. The godlessness of the world is "a clearing of the decks for the God of the Bible" —for the God not of worldly power, but of suffering.[35]

The Christian is, therefore, one who abandons all religious concerns and participates in the suffering of God in Christ. Suffering distinguishes the Christian from the heathen; it sets off the transcendent and faithful from the religious. Transcendence and faith require one to suffer, to participate in the Being of Christ, the Christ whose only concern is for others. In *Prisoner for God* Bonhoeffer says:

Our relation to God [is] not a religious relationship to a supreme Being, absolute in power and goodness, which is a spurious conception of transcendence, but a new life for others, through participation in the Being of God. The transcendence consists not in tasks beyond our scope and power, but in the nearest thing to hand. God in human form, not, as in other religions, in animal form—the monstrous, chaotic, remote and terrifying—nor yet in abstract form —the absolute, metaphysical, infinite, etc.—nor yet in the Greek divine-human of autonomous man, but man existing for others, and hence the Crucified.[36]

Suffering springs not from any religious aspiration, however noble it may be, but springs from the logic of the events

[75]

of the incarnation, cross, and resurrection of Christ. God identified himself through His Incarnation with the world—its happiness and sorrow, its success and failure, its goodness and evilness. And by this same token man ought to identify himself with the world. He ought to throw himself "utterly in the arms of God and participate in his sufferings in the world and watch with Christ in Gethsemane. That is faith, that is *metanoia,* and that is what makes a man and a Christian (cf. Jeremiah 45)." [37] The Christian is one who plunges himself "into the life of the godless world." "To be a Christian does not mean to be religious in a particular way, to cultivate some particular form of asceticism (as a sinner, a penitent, or a saint), but to be a man. It is not some religious act which makes a Christian what he is, but participation in the suffering of God in the life of the world." [38]

The Christian Church, Bonhoeffer declares, fulfills its true mission only as it exists for others. This is its reason for being. Its bounden duty is to sacrifice and serve, to be part of the world's suffering. The Church, insofar as it is zealous for self-aggrandizement, brings upon itself blame and shame. Preoccupied with its own life, it is mindless of the life of man. Perhaps what the Church needs is a fresh start. Possibly the Church should divest itself of all endowments and distribute them to the poor and the needy. And the clergy should forgo their professional stipends and live solely on the free-will offerings or the earnings of secular work. Every step must be taken so that the Church may recover its real purpose of telling men that the transcendent life is existence for others. The Church must speak of "moderation, purity, confidence, loyalty, steadfastness, patience, discipline, humility, content and modesty." [39]

This, then, is Bonhoeffer's case for the Christian faith without religion. His delineation is uneven and incomplete and remains open to all sorts of aberrational and overingenious speculation. Yet, his major thesis is unmistakable. The phenomenon of religion is strikingly absent from the modern man. The world is mature and free; the subterranean anxieties that once frightened the human soul have now been domesticated if not exterminated; man has, single-handedly, become their master. The Christian faith now stands alone, unfettered by a human longing for assuagement, and this is as it should be. For the God of the Christian faith is aristocratic. It is not His nature to ally himself with the importunities of despairing and sinful man. God comes to man in His own way and His own time, independent of and indifferent to man's religion.

CHAPTER 4 The Christian Faith as the Fulfillment of Religion: Friedrich Schleiermacher

FRIEDRICH SCHLEIERMACHER *was born in Breslau in November, 1768. During his early years he attended the Moravian school at Niesky, where he was deeply impressed by the Moravian spirit, and particularly by the Pietism of Zinzendorf. Later he enrolled in the Moravian theological seminary at Barby, an institution from which, because of his heterodox speculations, he was forced to take a premature departure. He went on to the University of Halle, and upon completing his theological education there, he became a minister of the Reformed Church. He served for a short while as a preacher and a domestic tutor in West Prussia. Later he accepted a teaching assignment at the University of Berlin and became the regular preacher in the city's Charity Hospital. The intellectual climate of Berlin was saturated with Romanticism, and Schleiermacher found living in this city to be very invigorating. The upshot was that the mental exhilaration, coupled with the encouragement of his friend, Friedrich Schlegel, brought Schleiermacher—in 1798 —to write his famous book,* ON RELIGION: SPEECHES TO ITS CULTURED DESPISERS. *Later, in 1804, he became a member of the faculty at Halle, where, in time, he taught the whole gamut of theological subjects except the Old Testament. In 1807 he returned to Berlin, first giving public lectures in Greek philosophy and preaching in the Holy Trinity Church, and later serving as a member of the staff of the new university in Berlin. Finally, in 1814, he was elected Secretary of the philological and historical section of the Academy of Berlin, a position which he held until his death in 1834. It was while he was with the Academy that he wrote his most important dogmatic work:* THE CHRISTIAN FAITH. *It was this work as much as any that distinguished Schleiermacher as the great herald of modern theology. His fresh delineation of Christianity helped prepare the European stage for Albrecht Kitschl, Ernest Troeltsch, Rudolph Otto, and others, and in America he was a theological progenitor of such liberals as Shailer Mathews, Eugene Lyman, and William Adams Brown. He is acknowledged (even by one of his most severe critics, Emil Brunner) to be one of the great theologians and great spirits of mankind.*

FROM ONE of Bonhoeffer's fellow countrymen and most distinguished predecessors comes another account of the relation between the Christian faith and man's religion. To begin with, this view presupposes that religion is a natural faculty of man, as natural as thinking and breathing, and that regardless of the contingencies of history and the fancies and feats of man, religion remains ineradicable. Also, it advances the idea that it is through the Christian faith that religion is brought to its state of full maturity. In other words, the Christian faith is upheld as the paragon of all religion; it is the completion of the incomplete religious concern of man. In Christianity, the God-consciousness, the religious solicitude of man, is ultimately fulfilled. This movement toward fulfillment, it is true, is a slow and gradual one, but, barring an unusual deficiency, fulfillment is virtually inevitable.

Thus spake Schleiermacher, the father of Protestant liberalism. Schleiermacher lived during the closing years of the eighteenth century and the opening years of the nineteenth century and was thoroughly acquainted with the intellectual world of his day. Throughout his theological career he lived and breathed the air of rationalism and the new science. Although he did not find all the elements of his intellectual world to be equally agreeable—in fact, some of them he found to be unpalatable—it was in the midst of this enlightened atmosphere that he gained his theological wisdom and stature.

Schleiermacher's theology is related to the thought of the Enlightenment in both a positive and a negative manner. The explanation for this twofold relationship revolves, in part, around the fact that one of the driving ambitions of the men of the Enlightenment was to codify all aspects of human existence—both ordinary and extraordinary, terrestrial and celestial—into intellectual systems and rational laws. The eighteenth century was, to quote D'Alembert, a "philosophic century par excellence." It was a time when everything was brought under the scrutiny of reason—theological issues, commercial affairs, metaphysical ideas, political matters. The institutions and ways of the Old Regime were, in the name of human intellect, roundly repudiated. A pervasive rational law, it was asserted, orders all human affairs, and the enlightened mind understands the law and applies it to the course of human events. Indeed, it was observed by some who witnessed the events of the day, the veneration of the power of reason is carried to such an extreme that it hardens into a creed. Turgot, who is by no means unsympathetic to the pre-eminence of reason, is reported to have complained that the *Encyclopedia*—the work which summed up the Enlightenment—is "the book of a sect." This objection may have been directed against the more extreme expressions of the rationalistic spirit and, therefore, not representative; nevertheless, there was throughout the day a common allegiance to the notion that the sum and substance of life is explicable within the categories of man's intellect.

Among the high causes to which the priests of the cult of rationalism dedicated themselves is that of restoring to religion its true meaning and dignity. They are concerned that the ideals and practices of faith be set free from all obscurant modes, allowing the spirit of man to thrive on its own "natural blessedness." In England, the deists of the seventeenth and eighteenth centuries, intent upon reducing Christianity to the "essentials," desire to make religion rationally defensible. On the Continent, Helvetius, Holbach, and others attack the citadels of ecclesiastical authority and denounce man's blind obedience to a heavenly potentate. As they see it, traditional Christianity, in its insipience, is hopelessly anachronous. Since all things are now examined through the scrutinizing eyes of reason, religion ought not make itself despicable by walking around in the outlandish garb of supernaturalism; religion, like its companions— economics, politics, and social relations—must be designed according to the fashionable intellectualism of the times.

Schleiermacher, as indicated above, is by no means at complete odds with the main currents of the Enlightenment. One point at which he heartily concurs with his contemporaries is the conviction that religion must be presented in a modern dress—that it must be made respectable so that it will gain the acclaim of "its cultured despisers." The presuppositions and tenets of religion, says Schleiermacher, must be dealt with in terms of the new thought; religion, in other words, if it is to gain approbation, must be sophisticated. Schleiermacher is prepared—in fact, he is eager—to dispense with many of the old doctrines and to help emancipate men from the deadening effects of dogma and ecclesiasticism. He insists that religion must not be allied with primitive superstitions, infallible oracles, and those supposedly sporadic, freakish occurrences within the universe which are commonly called miracles. The dogged and manifold encumbrances of religion must be thrown off. In the name of authentic faith, for example, scripture must not be defended any longer; for faith does not depend on scripture: scripture depends on faith. The orthodox doctrine of the inspiration of the Bible is without basis, says Schleiermacher, and he goes on to applaud, heartily, the "higher critics" of the Bible. Along with the rejection of the traditional view of scripture, Schleiermacher questions the conventional interpretation of miracles and prophecies. The accounts of these events in the scripture must not, he says, be construed as attestations to the authenticity of the Bible. In the main, Schleiermacher takes the position that there is nothing particularly mysterious about God's relationship with man, that God does not employ mechanical and magical measures to produce certain desired effects. On the contrary, the operations of God are open to the scrutiny of man, and there is an apparent continuity between the religious affections of man and the will and work of the Eternal God. In his unwillingness to support the orthodox position, Schleiermacher is not deliberately set upon repudiating the central message of the gospel, although, as we shall see, he actually did help bring about its superannuation. His primary ambition is to relieve Christianity of its odious accretions and, thereby, present it in a manner suited to the modern world. Insofar as Schleiermacher is possessed by this ambition, he stands side by side with the leaders of the Enlightenment.

Yet, in another sense, Schleiermacher's thought does run counter to the intellectual currents of his day. The philosophical attitude of the Enlightenment, which was designed to enliven and purify religion, has, says Schleiermacher, served to smother man's religious spirit. In the process of being intellectualized, religion has been devitalized. Faith, under the surveillance of reason, has become a matter of speculative arguments and of deductions from proof texts. Wittingly or unwittingly, the masters of natural theology have reduced religion to a barren rationalism and an arid metaphysics. To treat the articles of faith as if they were intellectual data to be reflected upon by a calculating mind is, says Schleiermacher, no different from the lonely man's equating his exciting theories about love with the experience of loving. Schleiermacher is convinced that the prevailing tendency to equate reason and religion is tantamount to the dissolution of true religion.

What is more, continues Schleiermacher, in the intellectualizing of religion, have the apostles of the Enlightenment actually improved upon the orthodox position? The rationalists have shouted loud and long against orthodox Christianity, and not without cause. At the time of the Reformation the theology of the Christian Church had been pried loose from Catholic scholasticism. But this new-found freedom was short-lived. The dynamic faith of Luther and Calvin was immediately supplanted by a mass of static formulas and statements of faith. There was a constant haggling over theological minutiae and interminable disputes over the subtleties of particular articles of faith. The man in the pew was required to give assent to certain dogmas and creeds. Belief in the *idea* that the Bible is the Word of God and the affirmation of the *doctrine* of predestination were regarded as evidences of true piety. It was against this absolutizing of doctrines and theories of the Christian faith that the men of the Enlightenment reacted, insisting that such inane practices would slowly but surely strangle the life out of all religion.

Yet, it is obvious, says Schleiermacher, that the rationalists are no better than their adversary. For the rationalists are no less guilty of reducing religion to a system of thought than are the orthodox theologians. The only difference is that the apostles of reason ground their thinking in the natural, while the prophets of orthodoxy rely upon the supernatural. Thus it is that Schleiermacher reacted not only against the Christianity of orthodoxy but also against the religion of the Enlightenment. For Schleiermacher the essence of true religion was neither doctrine nor reason—it was "feeling."

In addition to viewing Schleiermacher's theology against the background of the Enlightenment, attention should be given to three specific influences which helped shape his thought: Pietism, Immanuel Kant, and Romanticism. Within these are found some of the motifs which held a prominent place within his theology. The Pietistic movement began as a reaction against formalized and "theologized" expressions of religion in general and of German Lutheranism in particular. Among the distinguished leaders of this movement are Philipp Spener, August Francke, and Count Zinzendorf. It was especially through his familiarity with the thought of Zinzendorf that Schleiermacher came to appreciate the claims of Pietistic tradition. During his youth he attended the Moravian school in Niesky, an institution which was animated largely by the spirit of the beloved Zinzendorf. Later Schleiermacher enrolled in the Moravian theological seminary at Barby. Thus it was that Pietism made a lasting impression upon his thought, mostly in a positive way. The Pietists claim that to be truly religious is to experience the presence of Christ in one's heart. Their emphasis is upon the emotional, rather than the rational. Intellectual systems and right doctrines are regarded by the Pietists to be irrelevant; indeed, such concerns seem to insulate man from true religion. What is important, they say, is not theology or creed, but that the spirit of Christ bring about a change within the life of man. Man must be transformed inwardly. Through the presence of Christ, old things must be done away with and all things must become new. That man could truly ascend to the heights of the virtuous life is not seriously questioned by the Pietists. They do not look upon man as a depraved being, forever in rebellion against God. Their preoccupation is with the sanctified life. If a man is duly pious, it is believed, the spirit of Christ will reign in his heart, and he will sever his allegiance with all worldliness, giving himself only to that which is Christlike. The Pietists believe that the Kingdom of God is within, that it is in the subjective feeling of piety that one finds God and realizes the good life.

A second influence which made a deep impression upon Schleiermacher was Immanuel Kant. Kant, in one sense a child of the Enlightenment, is, at the same time, one of its most severe critics, exposing its weaknesses and helping to undermine its widespread appeal. In 1781 he published his epochal work, *The Critique of Pure Reason*, in which he makes the claim, among other points, that theoretical reason or pure reason is incapable of understanding things in themselves; it can only understand the things as they are experienced. In other words, the mind cannot know the "noumenal" reality, although such a reality is not to be denied; it can know only the "phenomena" which man experiences directly. In circumscribing the power of the human intellect by confining it to the realm of the human and the temporal, Kant delivers a severe blow to the high claims of rationalism. Philosophy and science do not, after all, have the last word on the nature of things divine. All the traditional arguments regarding the existence and nonexistence of God—indeed, all claims regarding a knowledge of God—are, according to Kant, so much batting of the air. Matters relating to the spirit cannot be contained within a comprehensive and intelligible order.

Having exposed the limits of "pure reason," Kant proceeds to explain the nature of another kind of reason—"practical reason." It is through practical reason, he says, that God and things belonging to Him must be accounted for. As far as Kant is concerned, theism is a valid theological position. Unlike Hume, who, having undermined the competence of speculative reason, concludes that the realm of the superhuman and supernatural must be rejected, Kant is unwilling to settle for the atheistic position. Simply because reason cannot yield knowledge about

God, he argues, it does not follow that there is not another way whereby God can be known. There *is* another way, said Kant: man apprehends God through the practical experience of the moral law within. Knowing God is based upon an experience of the heart. There is within every man a sense of duty, a moral consciousness which impels man to live the good life—a "categorical imperative." Moreover, this sense of moral obligation is not without content. What is required of man is that he affirm the fundamental principle of the dignity and worth of human personality: that he "so act as to treat humanity, whether in thine own person or in that of another, in every case as an end withal, never as means only." [1] Kant's moral philosophy undercuts the very foundations of the prevailing rationalism. With candor and cogency, he exposes the frailty of all speculative thought, showing its inability to speak of God, immortality, and freedom. If man is to speak of the Ultimate, concludes Kant, he must begin not with pure reason, but with the subjective consciousness of the moral law.

A third influence which helped to shape Schleiermacher's thought is Romanticism. The Romantic movement flourished when Schleiermacher was living, and, among the initiates of the movement, Schleiermacher was regarded as one of its "spiritual brethren." What is Romanticism? "It is man's return to himself," writes Robert Wernaer, "to one of the well-springs of his life, to the receptive, noncritical, emotional side of his nature. Romanticism is the cultivation of the free world of the spirit in art and life. And this free world of the spirit had its well-springs in man's heart always." [2] The champions of the Romantic movement insist that "the heart is the key to the world." The intellect, they claim, tends to suffocate the vital and dynamic strivings of the human spirit. Man is a being of passion, enthusiasm, faith, and love. The extent to which these qualities do and should sway the human soul was something of a moot issue. Should the emotional surgings of man go completely unrestrained? Although it was generally conceded that a rampant emotionalism is without justification, it was agreed that the experience of the heart must take precedence over the calculations of the intellect. Moreover, it should be noted that within the German Romantic movement it was widely believed "that the individual emotional life has its root in the Divine." Friedrich Schlegel declares that only that which is linked with the eternal has meaning and value. And in keeping with this assertion is Novalis's pronouncement that if eternity is not in man, then it is not found anywhere. The Romanticists assume that there is a divine personality outside of man which sustains and is identified with the human spirit. Ostensibly, many of the Romanticists claim allegiance to the transcendent God of Biblical faith. Yet, in actuality, among the German Romanticists there is a strong tendency to discard the transcendent God of the Bible for the immanent God of pantheism. It is the judgment of Robert Wernaer that for the Romanticists "God was, in part, of man's own making, not, as heretofore, the exclusively revealed and adopted Biblical God." [3]

Pietism, Kant, and Romanticism—these are three of the many influences which helped to mold Schleiermacher's thought, especially his interpretation of the Christian faith. Although these influences have been treated sketchily here, they do help point to some of the basic motifs which animated Schleiermacher's theology. The reliance upon subjective experience rather than upon reason, the dependence upon the testimony of the human heart rather than upon the revelation through Jesus Christ—these are some of the ideas which found their way into Schleiermacher's theological formulations.

Schleiermacher's venture into theology begins with a consideration of the nature of religion. What is its scope, its complexion, and its essential quality? In his book, *On Religion,* he reminds the nonbelievers that their effort to estrange themselves from spiritual matters is an entirely futile project. Religion is as old as the human race and is here to stay; it is a part of the human spirit. It is an element within the human soul; it is inseparable from the impulses of man's very being. Man harbors two basic impulses: on the one hand, the human self strives "to establish itself as an individual. For increase, no less than sustenance, it draws what surrounds it to itself, weaving it into its life, and absorbing it into its own being." On the other hand, the self is involved in the "dread fear to stand alone over against the Whole, the longing to surrender oneself and be absorbed in a greater, to be taken hold of and determined." [4] These two impulses stand in juxtaposition to each other, and, since religion involves the self in its relationship to the universe and particularly its desire to surrender itself, they are the occasion for all spiritual longings and enterprises. Thus, the existence of religion does not depend upon any condition extraneous to human nature; it is an attribute of man *ab origine,* and, whether it is or is not cultivated, it obstinately persists.

And the essence of religion is the "feeling of piety." Religion is a feeling wherein "those pious exaltations of the mind in which all other known activities are set aside or almost suppressed, and the whole soul is dissolved in the immediate feel-

ing of the Infinite and Eternal." [5] In religion man is at one with
God. Through the feeling of a contemplative and devout mind
the eternal content of life is fused with the human soul. Religion "is the immediate consciousness of the universal existence of all finite things, in and through the Infinite, and of all
temporal things in and through the Eternal." To be religious
"is to have life and to know life in immediate feeling." [6]
Schleiermacher appropriated the Romanticists' idea that the
Rationalists were grossly in error: it is an impugnation of truth
to conclude that the profundities of human existence can be
contained in the shallow receptacles of reason. After all, the
systems of rationalism are nothing more than "the handiwork
of the calculating understanding, wherein only by mutual
limitation each part holds its place." [7]

The facets of human personality include knowing, doing,
and feeling, but the greatest of these is feeling. It cannot be
otherwise. If religion were equated with knowing, the masters
of theology would be the most religious persons, but (God
knows!) this is not the case. If religion were synonymous with
doing, the energetic crusader would be supremely religious,
but, since activity can be both admirable and abominable, this
criterion is also inadequate. Underlying both knowing and doing is the feeling of piety. The knowledge of God and all doctrinal formulas "have their ultimate ground so exclusively in
the emotions of the religious self-consciousness [of piety], that
where these do not exist the doctrines cannot arise." [8] And, in
the same way, action is dependent upon feeling so that activities are pious to the extent that their underlying motivations
are pious. The feeling of piety is not extraneous to knowing
and doing, for, says Schleiermacher, "there are both a Knowing

[91]

and a Doing which pertain to piety, but neither of these constitutes the essence of piety." Knowledge and action are secondary to piety itself. Piety exists in its own right so that "no one will deny that there are states of Feeling, such as penitence, contrition, confidence, and joy in God, which we pronounce pious in themselves, without regard to any Knowing or Doing that proceeds from them." [9] In summarizing Schleiermacher's idea of piety, Professor Mackintosh writes:

> Schleiermacher obviously desires to secure the full independence of piety, as the soul's inner holy of holies, over against knowledge and morality. Quantity of knowledge, as he says, is not quantity of religion. Doubtless religion may take the form of contemplation, and has an open sense for the life of the world. But such contemplation does not view the individual object in the light in which science views it, i.e., as it stands related to other things, but in its character as a revelation of the infinite Unseen. What is specifically religious needs no certificate from knowledge; it carries with it the evidence of its own truth and shines by its own glow.[10]

So, then, the highest and noblest thing which can happen to the human soul is to experience the feeling of piety.

The experience of piety is passive rather than active, Schleiermacher argues. It is a state wherein the soul is grasped by an awareness of dependence, by a simple and complete dependence on God. In piety man senses that he is unconditionally dependent upon the world beyond himself. The pious man does not theorize, nor perform, but, as Rudolph Otto explains, is "sitting quietly in a corner," experiencing life in "receptive contemplation." [11] The consciousness of being absolutely dependent is the quintessence of true religion: man experiences a sense of humility toward the universe and toward

[92]

the totality of being, from which man and all things have originated. Man is aware that he is a part of the whole of life; the reality of the Absolute is part of his consciousness, and he knows that all life comes from a source outside the self. As has already been pointed out, the religious state is by no means foreign to human nature, for in every moment of self-consciousness the human soul is pulled by two opposing impulses: the desire for independence and the longing for dependence. It is the latter—the stronger of the two—which is the root of all religion.

So much for Schleiermacher's interpretation of religion. Now, in what way is the Christian faith the fulfillment of religion? Schleiermacher's formal definition of the Christian faith is as follows: *"Christianity is a monotheistic faith, belonging to the teleological type of religion, and is essentially distinguished from other such faiths by the fact that in it everything is related to the redemption accomplished by Jesus of Nazareth."* [12] To all appearances, this definitive statement is not a deviation from traditional Christianity. Is not the term "redemption," for example, a solid and upright orthodox term? Indeed, Schleiermacher's entire volume, *The Christian Faith,* and particularly its pages on Christology, are replete with the revered words and expressions of orthodoxy. For example, we read: *"participation in the Christian communion"* comes only *"through faith in Jesus as the Redeemer."* [13] *"The Redeemer assumes the believers into the fellowship of His unclouded blessedness. . . ."* [14] It is through Christ's "sinless perfection" that men are redeemed.[15] And, it is explicitly stated, Jesus is not to be regarded as a great teacher or reformer, but "is distinguished from all others as Redeemer alone and for all, and is in no wise regarded

as having been at any time in need of redemption Himself."
He was "separated from the beginning from all other men, and
endowed with redeeming power from His birth." [16]

But the exact nature of Schleiermacher's Christology is by
no means unambiguous. Is Christ to be explained as a miracu-
lous figure, or is He to be accounted for through the more natural, evolutionary processes of life? This is the difficulty. On the
one hand, Schleiermacher strongly suggests that Christ's perfection—the distinctive character of His life—defies a purely
human explanation; His complete sinlessness calls for a supernatural reading. On the other hand, Schleiermacher is careful
not to leave the impression that Christ's perfection distinguishes Him radically from other men; while Christ alone may
have attained perfection, His capacity for this state of goodness is not peculiar to Him alone. As Professor Mackintosh
puts it, "that perfection is a miracle, certainly, in the sense that
no other similar fact has occurred in history; it is not, however,
an absolute breach of man's normal development, for sin is not
part of essential humanity." [17]

The real weight of Schleiermacher's interpretation of
Christ seems to be on the side of a natural, evolutionary explanation. Christ is regarded as the archetype of piety. He is
the perfect manifestation of religion, the first person to incarnate fully the feeling of absolute dependence. He represents the culmination of the spiritual development toward
which the human race has been steadily moving. A supernatural account of Christ is unnecessary; the superiority of
Christ lies in His capacity to control and manifest His God-
consciousness. Of course, in some instances, Schleiermacher
seems to strike a more orthodox note; for example, he says:

"The Redeemer is like all men in virtue of the identity of human nature, but distinguished from them all by the constancy of His God-consciousness, which was a veritable existence of God in Him." [18] But, the last phrase notwithstanding, Schleiermacher disallows the conclusion that Christ is essentially different from other men. Christ is the true example of God-consciousness, a consciousness "which in Him too, as in all [other men] had to develop gradually in human fashion into a really manifest consciousness." [19] The gravity of Schleiermacher's thought is that Jesus is the one who, through the extension and intensification of His spiritual predilections, exemplified true piety and that God can be in man *in the same manner* in which He is in Christ. Christ and man belong to essentially the same category. Christ is the manifestation of true piety, the piety which to a greater or lesser extent is found in every human soul. Professor William Adams Brown seems to have caught the essence of Schleiermacher's view. "The moral qualities and influences on which Jesus relied during his earthly ministry," writes Brown, "are seen to be those which are most characteristically divine; and the proof of His uniqueness is found less in his ability to use supernatural means not open to His fellows than to the extent to which He showed Himself master of the moral and spiritual influences to which the deepest in man responds." [20]

By virtue of the excellence of Christ's God-consciousness, Christ is the revelation of God. That is to say, He is the revelation in the sense that He communicates his God-consciousness to others. Through the perfection of His God-consciousness He possesses the power to quicken man's God-consciousness; ". . . the God-consciousness already present in human nature,"

[95]

Schleiermacher explains, "though feeble and repressed, becomes stimulated and made dominant by the entrance of the living influence of Christ." [21] Because of his nature, man possesses an awareness of God apart from Christ; this original awareness is the correlate of man's natural sense of dependence. In the "original revelation" of God to man, Schleiermacher says: ". . . along with the absolute dependence which characterizes not only man but all temporal existence, there is given to man also the immediate self-consciousness of it, which becomes a consciousness of God." [22] Yet, in this original state the God-consciousness is "evinced only casually in isolated flashes, never kindling to a steady flame." [23] It is through Christ that "life comes under a different formula, making it a life that is new; hence the phrases 'a new man,' 'a new creature,' which bear the same sense as our phrase 'a new personality.'" [24] In the witness of Christ's God-consciousness man knows true piety. Seemingly, Schleiermacher would concur with Shailer Mathews' idea that Christ was "a sample of salvation"; ". . . once sharing in his [Jesus's] own sense of God, in his experience we are like him. We too shall find the Father." [25]

All in all, Schleiermacher's interpretation of revelation is a deviation from the classical Christian affirmation that Christ is the final disclosure of the infinite wisdom and love of God, the one through whom God judges the prideful pretentiousness of man and delivers man from despair and sin. Christ, for Schleiermacher, is a revelatory figure, but essentially in the sense that his God-consciousness empowers him to transform the lives of others.

Like Erich Fromm's, Schleiermacher's thought is strongly

reinforced by a belief in the goodness of man. Man is conceived in a state of goodness, Schleiermacher contends, and he maintains this high state throughout his entire life. Man is not a fallen creature, as orthodoxy claims. Derangements, disruptions, and the devil are alien impostors, in no way real components of the human soul. There is no serious gap between man and God. The aspirations harbored by the human personality are fundamentally Godly, and all that is called for is to realize them according to the Christian pattern. In a straight-forward manner, Schleiermacher rejects the idea that through Adam all men are permanently tainted with inordinate self-interest. He insists that this low estimate of man, like all the other disparaging views emanating from the fruit-eating episode in the Garden of Eden, must be permanently bequeathed to antiquity. Essentially, the conflict between good and evil is nothing other than the struggle of the spirit and the flesh: the flesh, or sense consciousness, checks the growth of the spirit, or God-consciousness. And the cunning and devious skill of the flesh to hamper the performance of the spirit must not be minimized. Yet, man is the crown of the universe, and the portrayal of him must be appropriate to his noble stature. His natural condition of goodness, his inherent disposition toward true piety—these constitute the true descriptions of man. What is more, the truth is not stretched in the claim that man is potentially perfect; there is no innate impediment which necessarily limits man to a status less excellent than that attained by Christ, the perfect Man. Evil is a part of the life of man, it is true, but this is not something positive in itself. Evil is only a *defect*—identified with the flesh—in man's ability to control the feeling of God-consciousness; evil is simply that which "has arrested the free development of the God-consciousness." [26]

Thus, Schleiermacher insists that the magnified accounts of man's imperfection as effused by the Biblical literalists and traditional theologians must be promptly dismissed. And while his own discussion of human nature is daubed with the traditional, well-worn terms, "original perfection" and "original sin," they take on a decidedly uncanonical hue. "Original perfection" refers to man's potential ability to develop perfect piety, and "original sin" signifies the obstructions which hamper man's attainment of "original perfection." Schleiermacher points out that his own account of sin "as an arrestment of the determinative power of the spirit, due to the independence of the sensuous functions, is certainly reconcilable with those explanations which describe sin as a turning away from the Creator," and then he adds, "though less so with those which interpret sin as a violation of the divine law." [27] The phrase "though less so" is infinitely short of being a hyperbole. Anything more thorough than a cursory examination of Schleiermacher's thought does not give the slightest inkling that he accepted the idea of sin as "a violation of the divine law" or the idea of an accompanying sense of guilt and condemnation and the longing for forgiveness.

Still another way whereby Schleiermacher upholds man's perennial goodness is by pointing to the natural affinity of man with man. Human beings, he claims, are not intrinsically set against each other any more than they are set against God. The incentive to give oneself to his fellow men is not imposed from without. Genuine love is a part of man's native equipment. Of course, disharmony occurs within human relationships because of misunderstandings and unfriendly acts, but this fact does not mean that the heart of man is consumed by a divisive egotism. On the contrary, the heart is unblemished and is set on living for others. Love for one's fellow man is, in fact, a cognate of the feeling of dependence. In this feeling, man impulsively desires to surrender himself to the Infinite —he longs to get rid of himself. And by virtue of the same psychological impetus he also seeks to lose himself in the lives of his fellow men. The two experiences—loss of self in the Infinite and in man—go hand in hand. Both occur because of man's consciousness of the unity of life, because of his desire to identify himself with the Infinite. In keeping with this line of reasoning, Schleiermacher explains that in our consciousness of the Infinite we are not aware "of ourselves as individuals of a particular description, but simply of ourselves as individual finite existence in general; so that we do not set ourselves over against any other individual being, but, on the contrary, all antithesis between one individual and another is in this case done away." [28] The fusion of man with God and the fusion of man with man are one and the same thing.

This perfect state of selflessness has been attained only by Jesus. Through the expansion of His life He became the lover of all humanity. His sympathy went to all persons, and He became completely identified with them; His love for others was so dominant that personal considerations disappeared. "Of course," writes Schleiermacher, "it was first through Christ (as Founder of a society which is capable of embracing all men, and which, while attaching individuals to itself, looks simply to the fact of their being human) that the racial consciousness, along with the God-consciousness and with the same object in view, has become a powerful practical motive." [29] But, again, it must be remembered, the achievement of Jesus does not lie outside the range of human possibilities. Jesus moved from sympathy to more sympathy, from unity to more unity, and nothing within man's make-up precludes him from duplicating the way of Jesus.

Whether right or wrong, Schleiermacher's optimistic view of the nature of man represents a break with traditional Christianity. For him, sin does not have the obstinacy and the depth which Christianity has long maintained that it has. Assuming the influence of Jesus, "human nature, repeating itself identically through heredity in every human being, is seen to be sufficient" for the actualization of the perfect piety.[30] The nature of man, including his manifestations of evil, warrants no radical alteration of human personality. Man's original character is virtuous and through the example of Jesus ought to be nurtured that it may be fully ripened.

One last question: What is the nature and status of God in Schleiermacher's thought? At one time he asserted that God signifies "that which is the co-determinant" in the feeling of absolute dependence and the one "to which we trace our being in such a state." [31] Thus, it appears that God is a reality who invokes the feeling of dependence; in this feeling, man knows God as the "whence" of his existence. But, here again, we encounter certain difficulties; Schleiermacher's view of God is not as clear-cut as the definition may suggest.

Schleiermacher employs the classical Christian terms to describe the Divine Being. God is Eternal. This assertion means that He is beyond all time and is the ground of all that is temporal. He has Himself neither a beginning nor an ending because He transcends all categories of time. God is Omnipresent. He is beyond all space and the cause of all that is spatial. He is not limited as is man by the dimensions of here or there, above or below. God is Omnipotent. He is the cause of all that is, the totality of all nature. God is Omniscient. He knows the relationship of the whole to the individual, for His knowledge of all things is absolutely complete. These then are the four main attributes of God. But what do the terms *really* mean? What about God's existence and His place in the subjective experience of piety? This question does not yield an easy answer. Briefly, the issue runs like this. On the one hand, Schleiermacher indicates that he expects his statements to be taken literally—i.e., to designate an objective reality which possesses these attributes. This meaning is implied in what he has said about *"the consciousness of being absolutely dependent, or, which is the same thing, of being in relation with God."* [32] So here it seems that he is not simply employing poetic language to describe a subjective feeling, but that he is referring to a reality different from the experience itself. And again, when commenting on the nature of the feeling of dependence, he writes: ". . . in the first instance God signifies for us simply that which is the co-determinant in this feeling and to which we trace our being in such a state; and any further content of the idea must be evolved out of this fundamental import assigned to it." [33] This is a way of saying that God is "the *Whence* of our receptive and active existence." [34] God is the Other to which we trace the origin of our particular religious feeling.

On the other hand, Schleiermacher casts an entirely different light on this matter when he declares that the attributes of God—Eternalness, Omnipresence, Omnipotence, and Omniscience—actually ". . . correspond to nothing real in God." [35] They are, he says, nothing more than human reflections upon the subjective religious experience. God and the trinitarian formula, for example, are poetic expressions and must not be taken literally; they are really *"accounts of the Christian religious affections set forth in speech;"* [36] *"All attributes which we ascribe to God are to be taken as denoting not something special in God, but only something special in the manner in which the feeling of absolute dependence is to be related to Him."* [37] Thus, it seems, all theological formulations are about human feelings, not about God. Doctrine is not the articulation of the Word of God, it is the description of the religious experience.

Yet, to terminate the discussion at this point is to avoid a fact which should be recognized: Schleiermacher's insistence that statements about God "correspond to nothing real in God" actually represents an effort to preserve the absoluteness of God. His point is that what men say about God must never be equated with God himself; the qualities of personality which we ascribe to God are always inadequate since God is a super-personal being. There is a sense in which Schleiermacher shares Paul Tillich's concern that God must always be thought of as the "God above god."

Nevertheless, whatever Schleiermacher's intentions may have been, his delineation of the nature of God tended to encourage the idea that man's theological statements about God are only expressions as to how man feels about God; doctrinal statements must be treated psychologically and not meta-physically. Perhaps if Schleiermacher had taken "revelation" more seriously, his preoccupation with the subjective aspect of faith would have been duly restrained. But it is precisely this lack of seriousness which helps fortify the attacks against his emphasis on the subjective experience. When viewed in the light of the Protestant reformers, who relied wholly on the Word, Schleiermacher seems to sanction a faith which begins not with God but with man. The fact is that during the earlier, more brash days of his theological ponderings he had tried to make religion appealing to those who despised it by informing them, in his first edition of On Religion, that the idea of God is not as "high and important" as many people think it is. That is to say, God is really not essential to true religion. (Later, when he re-edited his book, lest he incur the wrath of his fellow-Christians, he deleted this shocking statement.) While his later work, The Christian Faith, is theologically superior to On Religion, the emphasis on the subjective feeling of piety con-tinues to haunt its pages. Immediate consciousness, the move-ment of the soul within itself, the feeling of dependence—it is by no means obvious that these are not the primal and con-stant loci of his theology. So it is not without reason that those who view Schleiermacher's theology in terms of orthodoxy are inclined to argue that what he really does is to stuff the Bibli-cal God into a box and then stand on the lid and vigorously proclaim that what is essential is not God but religion. Much more could be said about Schleiermacher's conception of God, but, granted the ambiguity of his thought, the point of first importance is still evident: the God of the Christian faith is one who, in keeping with the preceding explanations of Christ, revelation, and man, symbolizes the continuity between man's religion and the Christian faith.

This, then, is the way Schleiermacher conceived the Christian faith to be the fulfillment of religion. Christianity is religion par excellence. Christianity is the religion in which Christ realizes the religious element in its primitive purity, in which Revelation is the verbalization of the insights of the human spirit, and in which man suppresses his ungodly designs, thereby allowing the spiritual and loving nature of man to prevail. The Christian faith intensifies and clarifies and purifies the natural and universal piety inherent in all religion. Christ does not represent something which is foreign to man; the Christian faith is not alien to man's religion. The American preacher, Phillips Brooks, whose theology was conceived within the Schleiermacherian tradition, is in a sense paraphrasing his master when he writes: "What is religion as it stands in relation to all our human life? Is it the contradiction, the denunciation, the destruction of it all? No, but it is the highest reach of our human life. There is nothing in religion, there is nothing in Christianity, which has not its roots in human nature, and in the fundamental affections of mankind. Utterly swept out of our thought must be an old contradiction between the graces of the gospel and the natural affections: the natural affections reach upward, and when they find the God who has been in them from the beginning, then they are the Christian graces." [38] Schleiermacher may not have used Brooks's words, but he seems to agree with the spirit of his thought.

CHAPTER 5 The Christian Faith as the Judgment Against Religion: Karl Barth

KARL BARTH *was born in May, 1886, in Basel, Switzerland. He studied at the universities in Bern, Berlin, Tübingen, and Marburg, and it was at the last-named institution that he came under the influence of Wilhelm Herrmann, his "unforgettable teacher." During his early twenties he assisted Martin Rade on the religious paper* DIE CHRISTLICHE WELT. *In 1909 he took charge of the German Reformed Congregation in Geneva, and two years later he became pastor in the village of Safenwil, in Canton Aargau. It was while he was in Safenwil that he questioned the strength of the liberalism that he had gained during his university days. Liberalism now impressed him as being too unrealistic and weak to sustain either himself or the members of his congregation. He felt the need for something more substantial. What could he preach? He wanted to find his ". . . way between the problem of human life on the one hand and the content of the Bible on the other." He wanted ". . . to speak to the people in the infinite contradiction of their life, but to speak the no less infinite message of the Bible. . . ."* [1] *In the midst of this quandary Barth re-examined the Bible, and the Book of Romans in particular. As a result of his serious study he wrote his commentary on* THE EPISTLE TO THE ROMANS *(completed in 1919), a work which was epochal, not only in the life of Barth, but also within the life of the Christian Church. In 1921 he moved from the pastorate to the university, teaching at Göttingen, Münster, Bonn, and Basel, in that order. Today the world-famous theologian is living in Basel, dividing his time between teaching at the university and completing his voluminous work on church dogmatics (a monumental production which deserves a place on the shelf with Calvin's* INSTITUTES*). Barth is beyond any doubt one of the theological giants of the present day; his thundering proclamations have shaken the entire Protestant world.*

THE CONTEMPORARY THEOLOGIAN Karl Barth offers a perspective on the Christian faith and religion which is as remote from Schleiermacher's as the Arctic is from the Antarctic. Barth agrees with his "liberal" adversary that no man is without some form of religion. He observes that every human being bows before some deity and that all men are concerned about the meaning of life, about "the world's beginning and end, the origin and nature of man, moral and religious law, sin and redemption." [2] But, from this point, in a voice no less resounding than the trumpets of Jericho, trinitarian Barth shouts No! No! No! to everything which Schleiermacher says.

[106]

"With all due respect to the genius shown in his work," declares Barth, "I can*not* consider Schleiermacher a good teacher in the realm of theology because, so far as I can see, he is disastrously dim-sighted in regard to the fact that man as man is not only in *need* but beyond all hope of saving himself; that the whole of so-called religion, and not least the Christian religion, shares in this need; and that one cannot *speak* of God simply by speaking of man in a loud voice." [3] (That there have been occasions when Barth has spoken more kindly of Schleiermacher is not to be overlooked.[4] But the fact remains that it is Barth's more acrimonious charges against Schleiermacher that represent the real thrust of his attack against liberalism and provide a clear delineation of the idea that the Christian faith is a judgment against religion.)

Barth's theology represents a violent reaction against the spirit of the Enlightenment. In his thundering proclamations, he decries the rationalism and moralism of modern man, insisting that these humanistic developments are an unmitigated denial of what is at the heart of the Christian faith. Man is, says Barth, endeavoring to make himself God. He arrogantly assumes that everything revolves around himself, instead of around God. "We have lost the wonder of *God*," shouts Barth, "and now we have to learn to eke out an increasingly difficult and miserable existence by asserting the wonder of the *world*, the miracle of history and of the inner life (all equally questionable!)." [5] The modern philosophical movement, as inaugurated by Descartes, has crowned man with the power to rule himself. With the advent of the Age of Reason, the Absolute has been replaced by the relative, and truth has been reduced to "moral and sentimental maxims." All in all, man now lives in a world wherein the theonomy of Christianity has been supplanted by the autonomy of the Enlightenment.

Although Barth does not hesitate to heap scorn upon the general spirit of the Enlightenment, the chief object of his caustic criticism is the Christian Church. In the Church's effort to reconcile the gospel with modern thought, Barth declares, it has succumbed to a subjectivism which is totally incompatible with the faith as revealed in the Word of God; the life-giving elements of Reformation theology have been replaced by the humanistic motifs of modernism. Emil Brunner, in 1928, is speaking not only for himself but also for his friend—friend at that moment, that is—Karl Barth, when he says: "Gradually the Biblical dualistic concepts were replaced by a progressive, monistic, and optimistic idealism; the Biblical doctrines of salvation and revelation, by Stoic and Platonic ideas. The 'Son of God,' the Messiah, was changed into a religious genius and hero: *creatio ex nihilo* became *creatio continua,* i.e., evolution; salvation was identified with religious behavior and ethical betterment; judgment and forgiveness were resolved into subjective values of a sentimentally religious kind." [6] What has happened to the theology of the Church! The hymn-singing and preaching have become idolatrous: the sovereignty of God has become the sovereignty of man. Christian theologians, like the humanists of the Enlightenment, proceed to build faith upon human experience; they have lost sight of the tragic dimension of man's existence and of the infinite abyss which exists between man and God. In place of the "Word of God" we now have "words of illumination." In succumbing to the cultural religion of the modern times, the Church has lost its saving

Word; in embracing the reasonable world of the rationalist, it has given up its true reason; in subscribing to the relativism of the new science, it has sacrificed its objective reality. Theology has degenerated into a meditation and concentration upon a truth which springs from man himself. Faith has become entirely personal, individualistic; God has become a projection of man's thoughts and feelings.

And the criticisms that are hurled against the Christian Church in general are, observe several German thinkers, poignantly applicable to the Church of Barth's own country. Liberalism has struck at the Church in Germany, reducing it to a state of spiritual infirmity. Count Keyserling reports his observation that "There is no longer any Church since Luther's day in evangelical Germany. It is but a form of life of the German sort (i.e., purely nationalistic)." [7] Adolf Allwohn is convinced that in Germany "preaching has degenerated into becoming a scientific discourse and at best is but a setting forth of the general truths of reason; worship has been thrust out of its central position to the periphery, and the church has become a society for religious-ethical culture, the sign of which is that instead of *God's* House there has been substituted a social centre." [8] Barth, too, is acutely aware of the need to put his own household of faith in order. The Church in Germany, he says, is too much concerned about culture and religion and too little concerned about the gospel. In view of this fact, he goes on to ask, what is the sense of all the "preaching, baptizing, confirming, bell-ringing, organ-playing, of all the religious moods and modes." Are not the pious exercises and elaborate programs only so much ado about nothing? It is no wonder, says Barth, that the churches are empty. People come hoping that the Church will speak of that which is ultimately important, of the Word. But what happens? Instead of feeding them this bread of heaven it offers them the stone of the illuminated mind. Having been disillusioned, the people stay away from the Church, leaving it to itself and its timid and kindly formulas. Truly the Church has lost its savor.

How did the Church come to this perilous state? What influences are responsible for bringing it to the fatal abyss of liberalism? Of course, a multitude of forces and conditions were at work, not the least of which was the impact of the Enlightenment upon the life and thought of the Church. But granted this obvious fact, what persons within the Church itself have played a major role in ushering in the new liberal theology? In answer to this question, Barth points out that standing high among the chief spokesmen of modern theology are Schleiermacher and Ritschl. Both of these theologians are bent upon harmonizing the gospel of Jesus Christ with the thought of the modern world. And what is the result? The baby is thrown out with the bath: in the process of making Christianity respectable the unique dimension of the gospel is discarded. Look at Schleiermacher! What has he done to Christianity? In trying to reconcile Christianity with the thought of the day, he represents God as immanent rather than transcendent, and equates revelation with the subjective experience of piety. Schleiermacher, says Barth, wants to connect heaven and earth in some amicable manner, thereby overcoming the dualism of Luther's theology. But, in his modern notion that all things must be happily joined together, the father of liberalism has placed the Christian faith beside all other religions; the unique and absolute dimension of the gospel is denied. If one begins with the Christian scheme of things, Schleiermacher's thought represents an inversion of the truth: he believes that God is to serve man and not man to serve God. In no way can Schleiermacher's thought be reconciled with the Christian faith. It is evident, concludes Barth, that "his Christology and his doctrine of atonements are clearly derived from his own experience of the human subject." What he has done is to reduce Christianity "to the hypothesis of being the highest expression of a religious instinct common to all men." [9]

Following Schleiermacher, and leaning heavily upon him, is Albrecht Ritschl. This eminent German theologian is, in the judgment of Barth, no less guilty than is Schleiermacher of dissolving the Christian faith in the acids of modernism. Ritschl claims, among other things, that the distinctive mark of Christianity is the ethical dimension—rather than the theological. Its primary purpose is, he believes, to render value judgments regarding the right relationship of man to the world. "Religious knowledge," writes Ritschl, "moves in the independent value judgments, which relate to man's attitude to the world, and call forth feelings of pleasure or pain, in which man either enjoys the dominion over the world vouchsafed him by God, or feels grievously the lack of God's help to that end." [10] It is this emphasis upon the ethical, incidentally, which became one of the dominant motifs of the "new theology" and the "social gospel" movements in America. Professor Waldo Beach reminds us that the priority of ethics over theology was one of the most radical features of the liberal movement. For the liberal mind the idea of the Kingdom of God was the vantage point before which all theology had to be judged. [11] For Ritschl, the notion of the Kingdom is the hub around which all Christian thought revolves, including the interpretation of Christ. The Kingdom, as he sees it, is not a complicated idea; it is simply "the union of subjects bound together by righteous conduct." It is essentially immanent rather than transcendent, horizontal rather than vertical. Assuming the primacy of the Kingdom, Ritschl explains that the secret of Christ's extraordinary power and goodness lies in His deliberate intention to become the founder of the Kingdom. In the exclusiveness of His devotion to His vocation, Christ becomes the kingly Prophet of the Kingdom, the one who overcomes the world. Christ is the "prototype" of the concept of the Kingdom of God; He is the "founder" of the Kingdom, the "inspiring force" which brings others to the Kingdom. He is the great Prophet who, through sheer determination, is able to educate and, thereby, transform His life for the sake of the Kingdom. All in all, Ritschl views Christ as a supremely good man, one whose excellence merits man's emulation.

But according to Barth's reasoning, Ritschl has not taken Christ and revelation seriously. In place of the Absolute Word of God, it is charged, Ritschl holds up the ethical teachings of Jesus. The central Christian affirmation that God has revealed Himself once and for all in Jesus Christ—this is not an integral part of Ritschl's thought. At this point Karl Barth and Dean Inge are in the same theological camp; Barth could not help approving Inge's reprehending statement: "The Jesus on whom he [Ritschl] makes the whole weight of his faith rest is merely the prophet of Nazareth in Galilee." [12] And Inge continues, ". . . we cannot help suspecting that this divinising of the Historical Jesus is consciously only a value judgment, and that religious truth for him is purely subjective."[13] What Ritschl is doing, according to Barth, is dispelling the light with darkness.

Barth, in renouncing Protestant liberalism, chose to find his theological anchorage within the more orthodox stream of thought. The tradition of the Reformed Church and the faith of Soren Kierkegaard—it was these influences, among many others, which helped him redefine his theological position. He came to a new appreciation of the historic affirmation of the Reformed Church—his own church—and concluded that it is within this tradition that one discerns the true nature of the faith. The central principle of Reformed theology is the Word of God: the Christian Church is born of, and abides in, the proclamation of the Word. The progenitor of Reformed theology, John Calvin, declares that the only way to seek God is *in* His Word; the only way to think of Him is *with* His Word, and the only ways to speak of Him is *through* His Word. According to Calvin, says Barth, God is totally other than man. God is infinite while man is finite; He is good while man is evil—so evil, in fact, that he can do nothing about his salvation. God, the Almighty and Everlasting God, acts, rules, redeems through His Word. "At their very beginnings," observes Barth, "the Reformed churches saw that truth is contained only in the word of God, that the word of God for them lay only in the Old and New Testaments, and that every *doctrine* must be measured against an unchangeable and impassable standard discoverable in the Scriptures." [14] It is on these Calvinistic pronouncements that Barth takes his stand.

Also, Barth acknowledges the influence of Kierkegaard upon his thought. In his introduction to his commentary on Romans, Barth takes time to point out: ". . . if I have a system, it is limited to a recognition of what Kierkegaard called the 'infinite qualitative distinction' between time and eternity, and to my regarding this as possessing negative as well as positive significance: 'God is in heaven, and thou art on earth.' " [15] Barth regards Kierkegaard's belief in the infinite distinction between God and man to be the central fact of all Biblical faith. God is God and man is man. All efforts to synthesize that which is of God with that which is of man is sheer blasphemy. Kierkegaard, fearful that he may attribute to God the predicates of human life, yet, of necessity, unable to leave God completely unnamed, chooses to call Him the Unknown—the "absolutely Unknown." In unison Kierkegaard and Barth exclaim: "God is the 'wholly Other.' " This is not to say that Barth concurs with Kierkegaard in every respect. There are differences. For example, Barth feels constrained to criticize the Danish existentialist's tendency to identify "God" with the "infinite." Barth's argument at this point is that Kierkegaard's conception of infinitude is simply that of timelessness and spacelessness and that, consequently, to speak of God as infinite is to reduce God to an "inner worldly dialectic." In other words, to talk about God as infinite is simply to talk about man, but negatively. Yet, granted this error on the part of Kierkegaard, Barth has a deep appreciation for the Danish theologian's exposition of the Christian faith; indeed, Barth's entire theology echoes Kierkegaard's claim: "God is in heaven, man upon earth; therefore they cannot well talk together."

Barth's theology is essentially "corrective"—i.e., it is intended to provide a corrective to the humanism that has flooded Christianity. He is pleading for the Church to return to its true mission, that of proclaiming the Word of God. In trying to stem the tide of liberalism, Barth seeks to gain his theological moorage by re-examining some of the more traditional affirmations of the Christian Church. He finds that it is in Kierkegaard, Calvin, Luther, Paul, and Jeremiah that one comes closest to the pristine purity of the gospel. It is, to a great extent, from these men that Barth derives the incentive and culls the insight which causes him to announce in unmodulated tones that the Word of God is infinitely different from the word of man, and that the Christian faith is the judgment against all man's religious consciousness.

Barth's polemic on religion and the Christian faith presupposes the religiousness of man. In his opinion, all men are aware of some overpowering force or condition which determines the destiny of their lives. From the most primitive to the most civilized levels of culture, men are aware of the awful powers of nature and of the inexorable operation of the spirits. "Human culture in general and human existence in detail," Barth writes, "seem always and everywhere to be related by men to something ultimate and decisive, which is at least a powerful rival to their own will and power. Both culture and existence seem to have been determined or partly determined by a reverence for something ostensibly more than man, for some Other or wholly Other, for a supreme Relative or even the Absolute." [16] What is more, the dominant motifs and chief practices of religion are essentially the same everywhere. Man in all times and places has taken it to be his duty "to offer worship to God or gods in the form of concrete cults: by occupying himself with pictures and symbols of deity, by sacrifice, acts of atonement, and prayers, by customs, games and mysteries, by the formation of communions and churches." [17] Everywhere the deities are compressed into images and pictures and held high as objects of worship. Religious groups everywhere possess "bibles," through which they endeavor to present the practices and the content of their particular tradition. The Indians have the Veda, the Persians have the Avesta, the Buddhists have the Tripitaka, the Christians have the Old and New Testaments; these holy books are supposedly endowed with authority and said to contain the last word concerning man's duties to the deities. All religions are concerned with the same problems and outlook. They are all preoccupied with the meaning of human existence, with the "why" of man's creation and the "wherefore" of his destiny. It is the enigma of human existence which causes man to solicit the favor of the gods. Man lives by the hope that through the proper relationship with the gods his predicament can be resolved and the soul can achieve a state of renewal and beatification.

But, in the name of the Christian faith, all religion, Barth insists, must be regarded as a totally unholy enterprise. For the true faith—the revelation of God—is totally other than religion. The ways of God are so infinitely different from man that all religious ingenuity and piety fall infinitely short of reaching God. According to Barth, God "stands *above* us and also above our highest and deepest feelings, strivings, intuitions, above the products, even the most sublime, of the human spirit." God is one who "in no way corresponds to a human disposition and possibility, but who is in every sense established simply in Himself and is real in that way." [18] Moreover, God is so infinitely different from all other gods that He cannot be set within the pantheon of other deities. He completely "takes the place," says Barth, "of everything that elsewhere is usually called

'God,' and therefore suppresses and excludes it all, and claims to be alone the truth." Moreover, "God in the sense of the Christian Confession is and exists in a completely different way from that which is elsewhere called divine. And so His nature, His being is different from the nature and being of all alleged gods." [19]

Barth's case for the "Otherness" of God cannot be overstated. God is, he argues, *absolutely* strange to all that is human. God resides beyond the range of human accessibility, completely different from anything that man himself can ever know. The wisdom of the Almighty is foreign to all the imaginations and pious stirrings of the human soul; He ordains a way of life that is entirely contrary to all human wisdom. There is not even a first step that man can take to move toward God. Man is abysmally distant from all that is Godly. Man cannot speak to God or of God; he can only wait for God to speak. In his *Dogmatics in Outline* Barth says:

What man can know by his own power according to the measure of his natural powers, his understanding, his feeling, will be at most something like a supreme being, an absolute nature, the idea of an utterly free power, of a being towering over everything. This absolute and supreme being, the ultimate and most profound, this "thing in itself," has nothing to do with God. It is part of the intuitions and marginal possibilities of man's thinking, man's contrivance. Man is able to think this being; but he has not thereby thought God. God is thought and known when in His own freedom God makes Himself apprehensible. . . . God is always the One who has made Himself known to man in His own revelation, and not the one man thinks out for himself and describes as God.[20]

God, the Other, has revealed Himself through Jesus Christ —the "Very God and Very Man." This means that Jesus Christ

[117]

is God who became flesh and dwelt among men. "'He who from eternity willed to become man for our good, has become man in time for our good, will be and remain man in eternity for our good'—that is, Jesus Christ." [21] Humanly speaking, this affirmation sounds preposterous, and Barth agrees with Dorothy L. Sayers when she says that if this strange fact were published in the newspaper it would be the most sensational story possible.[22] God, the Creator, has in his condescension come to man, the creature; God is present in our world, as a man among men. Christ is God and Man. All efforts to reduce Jesus Christ to a good man, or a great prophet, or a superb teacher, are sheer blasphemy; to speak of Jesus Christ in such humanistic terms is to talk about something other than revelation. The truth is this: ". . . God is this Man and this Man is God. . . ." [23] And in this startling fact alone lies man's salvation. It was in Jesus Christ that God turned to address man and to reconcile man with Him. God in his grace did for man what it was impossible for man himself to do: in the power of His love He cut the binding ties of sin that man might be united with Him.

God has come to man in Jesus Christ, so that man now knows what he himself could never know. Yet, while the divine word has come to man, the fact remains that this knowledge cannot be incorporated as a part of the human scheme of things. No, never! Revelation is forever that which is completely beyond anything that can be apprehended by human contemplation or reconciled with human thought. "It comes to us as a *Novum* which, when it becomes an object for us, we cannot incorporate in the series of our other objects, cannot compare with them, cannot deduce from their context, cannot regard as analogous with them." [24] Jesus Christ brings that which is totally alien to man. "It comes to us," says Barth, "as a datum with no point of connexion with any other previous datum. It becomes the object of our knowledge by its own power and not by ours." And, he goes on to say, "If we are aware of it and declare that it is true, we will also be aware and will not hesitate to declare, that it can be manifest to us in its truth only by its own agency and not because of any capacity belonging to us. . . ." [25]

In the light of revelation, all religion is unbelief, Barth argues; revelation informs man that God is Almighty, that He is the Lord of man and the source of *all* truth. In revelation man comes to know God and to know that the divine is altogether different from the human. Revelation proclaims that God is Lord and that He can be known only as He makes Himself known. In Barth's own words: "The truth that God is God and our Lord, and the further truth that we could know Him as God and Lord, can only come to us through the truth itself." [26] But it is precisely the sovereignty of God which the religious man will not accept. He tries to do what only God can do. He endeavors to anticipate what God has to say; he strives to reach toward God. He does not believe. Seemingly for Barth, the appropriate figure of faith is not man standing erect with outstretched hands waiting for God's revelation; rather, it is man with his head bowed and hands down, totally helpless to look toward God. In religion man talks; in revelation man listens. In religion man tries to give; in revelation man receives. All the religious inquiries and nice explanations of things eternal are a naked offense to God. Man must believe. "We need to renounce all attempts even to try to apprehend this truth. We need to be ready and resolved simply to let the truth be told us and therefore to be apprehended by it." [27]

In the light of revelation man is reconciled solely through the grace of God. Only through Jesus Christ can all things become new. "The revelation of God in Jesus Christ," writes Barth, "maintains that our justification and sanctification, our conversion and salvation, have been brought about and achieved once and for all in Jesus Christ." [28] Everything, absolutely everything, has been done once and for all through Jesus Christ. The Saviour takes all sin upon Himself. But again the religious man defies this saving work of God, for just as he tried to know God, so he tries to reconcile himself with God. He is not willing to trust God. He contradicts revelation by presuming that he can save himself. He tries to take his life into his own hands and to reach for God through worship, doctrines, and good works. He wraps himself in a cloak of piety and then presumes that his shining armor puts him right with the divine (and, of course, with his fellow men). He is not willing to have God accept him as he is; he wants to make himself acceptable. He is zealous about trying to be good and praiseworthy. Driven by the zeal to make something of himself, the religious man endeavors to multiply his good works, purify his worship, strengthen his doctrines. But, alas, Barth exclaims, all the piety in the world is of no avail. It is but another way in which man puts himself in opposition to God. "God in His revelation will not allow man to try to come to terms with life, to justify and sanctify himself." [29] And all efforts to do so only signify man's unbelief.

Barth is saying that, in essence, the fatal weakness of all religion is that it does not take seriously the infinite abyss between God and man. It denies that God is God and that man is man. It presumes that man is endowed with sufficient virtue to ascend to the lofty heights of the divine. Religion equates man with God. It imagines that God is nothing more than the disclosure of the supreme and best of that of which man has always had partial knowledge. It assumes that something of the divine is naturally contained within the human spirit. This is the logic on which religion is predicated. It accepts precisely what it should reject: that God is "a continuation and enrichment of the concepts and ideas which usually constitute religious thought in general about God"; that God is at the end of "the long road of human seeking and longing for the divine"; that "there is in humanity something like a universal natural disposition, a general concept of the divine, which at some particular point involves the thing which we Christians call God and as such believe in and confess." [30] Religion imagines that man is good and trustworthy, that he enjoys an affinity with God. Religion is too nonchalant about man's sin; it does not acknowledge that man is a fallen creature in whom the image of God has been utterly defaced. It ignores what the Bible clearly states: "Man has now become a tarnished mirror in which the glory of God can no longer be reflected." It does not recognize that it is not simply that man's actions are wrong —like crimes and immoralities—but that man's total being is set against God. "To be man," says Barth, "means *now* to be an enemy of God. . . ." [31] Man is spiritually impotent with no power whatsoever whereby he can realign himself with God. Man as man is wrecked, and all his efforts to salvage himself are entirely futile.

The passionate and pugnacious manner in which Barth

asserted man's depravity and estrangement from God is disclosed in his celebrated debate with Emil Brunner. Brunner at one time helped carry the Barthian standard, but "roughly since 1929" the Swiss theologian has gone his separate way. Finally, in 1934, warfare broke out between Brunner and Barth. The opening shot was Brunner's essay entitled "Nature and Grace," in which he explained his disagreement with Barth and summoned "our theological generation to find the way back to the true *theologia naturalis.*" [32] Brunner, intent on re-endowing man with the capacity of God, argued that revelation comes not only through Jesus Christ but through creation as well, and that although man is sinful he possesses the capacity to respond to "the divine grace of redemption." [33] And in taking this stand, Brunner claimed that he was fighting side by side with John Calvin. But to all this Barth fired back with a fast and angry: No! Brunner is said to be a traitor in that he has denied the reformer's principle of *sola gratia*—salvation through grace alone. And he is utterly wrong about the task of our theological generation; contrary to Brunner, says Barth, "we must learn again to understand revelation as *grace* and grace as *revelation* and therefore turn away from all 'true' or 'false' *theologia naturalis.*" [34] Brunner's idea of revelation of creation is called blasphemy; only in Christ does God reveal himself. Moreover, Barth complains, Brunner has employed the most unscrupulous means to advance his position: he has been "not content merely to hunt with the hounds and to stab me in the back" but has also "gone and calmly claimed Calvin for his own." [35] This is outrageous! Barth then proceeds to set things straight by pre-empting Calvin as a vigorous antagonist of natural theology. And to this end he cites Calvin's statement:

"The knowledge of God which now remains to man is nothing other than the terrible source of all idolatry and superstition." [36]

Man's religion, Barth says, is a most damnable enterprise. But this fact becomes evident only when religion is viewed in terms of the revelation of the Holy Scriptures. It is revelation alone which possesses the power and righteousness to expose religion for what it is. Religion itself cannot do this. Religion can, of course, call itself into question, but such a criticism is too feeble to expose the really idolatrous and self-righteous nature of religion. What happens when religion criticizes itself? For one thing we discover that religion is self-condemning. Religion, because of its very nature, struggles to move from the lower to the higher, from the good to the better, and, in the attempt to move upward, it must of necessity make judgments against itself. Yet, the judgments, while intended to be a salutary measure, turn out to be solely condemnatory. And secondly, religion is self-destructive in that it asks questions that it is not equipped to answer. It questions man's life, but is unable to provide the true way; it tears down but cannot build up.

At this point Barth anticipates that the apologists for religion may rejoin that, although the lower forms of religion may contain the fatal weaknesses mentioned above, these weaknesses are not peculiar to the higher forms. Barth accepts the challenge. And in reply he points out that *all* religion is self-contradictory by virtue of the fact that it is a useless enterprise, that it is "not necessary." Why is this true? Religion by its very nature is a phenomenon in which the inner aspirations of men are externalized—i.e., satisfied, represented, expressed. And, among other things, religion purports to fulfill man's need for truth. In other words, it believes that there is truth and that the truth is attainable. But it is at this point that the self-contradicting nature of all religion becomes evident. For is it not true that if man knows that there is truth he already possesses it, at least potentially? Thus is it not nonsense for a man to be searching for that which he already possesses? The religious man, Barth points out, "betrays the fact that even as he seeks satisfaction, potentially at least, in respect of his religious capacity he is already satisfied." He goes on to say: "The life of religion, in which religious need seeks satisfaction and provisionally finds it, is fundamentally only an externalization, an expression, a representation and therefore a repetition of something which previously existed without form or activity, but still quite powerfully, as the real essence of religion and to that extent as the peculiar religious possession of man." [37]

Moreover, says Barth, religion suffers from the fundamental weakness of being merely a reflection of what man already is, originally and internally. It is inevitable that religion cannot be anything other than what man already is; it is simply the satisfaction of an external need. And what becomes of the reflection if the religious man, the man originally and internally, changes? Should the reflection change with him? If religion changes as man changes, it becomes relative and must give up any claim to truth and certainty. If it does not change as man changes, it loses its relevance and becomes obsolete and fossilized. And if it chooses both possibilities—change and non-change—it incurs the advantages of both, but, to the same extent, takes on the twofold disadvantages as well. Religion has no way out of its malady, and that is why all religions are "acutely or chronically sick." [38]

The proponent of religion here interrupts and reminds

[124]

Barth that religion can be not only external but nonexternal as well—e.g., mysticism and atheism. Nonexternal religions are internal, formless, and unrealized; they are religion in the raw, so to speak. They do not try to go anywhere. They retain religion, but it is lived without expression and satisfaction. They are formless and require nothing. In nonexternal religions the vitality which man usually directs to the fulfillment of religion is turned inward in favor of the unactivated, the unthought, the unwilled. "The same acuteness of thought," Barth explains, "and the same power of will with which we once exerted ourselves positively and constructively, when we could still accept ourselves as religious believers, are now active negatively and destructively." [39]

Mysticism is the conservative expression of nonexternalized religion. It represents a withdrawal from the outward religion and a concentration on the inward, spiritual, vital meaning. The mystic is not an iconoclast who wants to get rid of religion; he is only a zealous searcher who is trying to reestablish the true locus of religion. He uses the argument "that everything external is only a form and picture, that the transitory is only a parable, that its truth is only in its relation to the inexpressible." [40] The mystical experience is one "of renunciation, of silence, of the way of quietude." [41] The only thing the mystic says about his experience is that nothing can be said; the only fact he signifies is that nothing can be signified. Yet, Barth warns, at least one fact must not be overlooked: while it is true that mysticism is a religion of renunciation, the crucial fact is that its existence is dependent upon that which it renounces. For what is left of mysticism if the externalization to which it objects is eliminated? Nothing—not even mysticism

—remains. The mystic needs the external religion because it is "the text of his interpretations," "the material for his spiritualizing." "It is the point of departure for the great withdrawal, on which, as he thinks, a knowledge of the truth will be achieved." [42] Mysticism thrives on "the glory of the vacuum which takes into itself everything outward." [43]

Atheism is the radical example of nonexternalized religion. It attempts to be completely iconoclastic, proclaiming loudly and bluntly that it is against all religion. God, dogma, the moral law—they must all be wiped out. But, says Barth, in this blatant and relatively unsophisticated repudiation of religion, atheism is on two counts less astute than mysticism. First, unlike mysticism, atheism is totally unmindful that its denial of religion is dependent upon the existence of religion and that if the latter condition were eliminated atheism would have to go too. Secondly, atheism naively reasons that when it has annihilated the traditional religious manifestations it has thereby wiped out all religions. It is unaware that there are dogmas, doctrines, and observances which are not necessarily allied with the usual religious expressions, but nevertheless assume a religious character. Indeed, do not such secular concerns as the primacy of reason, the fate of history, the reality of nature frequently take on ultimate devotion and sanctity? While atheism sweeps evil spirits out the front door, new and equally vicious demons are sneaking in the back one. At this point mysticism is much shrewder: it sweeps in all directions. The renunciations of mysticism are aimed not only at God but at the cosmos and the individual as well. Its concern is not with this or that display of religion but with any and every form of religion.

Mysticism and atheism are undeniably straightforward

and bold, but their efforts to dispose of religion are futile. They are too impotent to render the fatal blow because they are themselves too inextricably tied to religion: they need it for their own survival. And in addition, atheism, in slamming shut one religious door, only jars open another.

The real judgment against religion can never come from within; it must come from without—i.e., from the revelation in Jesus Christ. Through the vantage point of Christ it becomes apparent that all religion is a sham, a lie. And the phrase "all religion" is not inaccurate. For the Christian religion, too, apart from the redeeming grace of God, is a most damnable enterprise. And the strictures against religion must never be misconstrued as a denunciation of non-Christian religions and a concomitant exoneration of Christianity. To put Christianity in a category different from that of other religions is to miss the point entirely. Revelation judges and negates all religion, including Christianity. So it is the business of the Christian to take this judgment and apply it first and completely to himself. The judgment will be painful, of course. "This judgment means," Barth explains, "that all this Christianity of ours, and all the details of it are not as such what they ought to be and pretend to be, a work of faith, and therefore of obedience to the divine revelation. What we have here is in its own way— a different way from that of other religions, but no less seriously —unbelief, i.e., opposition to the divine revelation, and therefore active idolatry and self-righteousness." [44] The theology, doctrines, worship, morals, poetry, and arts of Christianity are, like all human phenomena, repudiations of God's revelation. The entire story of Christianity is one of betrayal and unfaithfulness; throughout Christian history the word of God has been

[127]

equated with the word of man: ". . . great and small Babylonian towers are erected, which cannot as such be pleasing to God, since they are definitely not set up to His glory." [45] Christians have pretended that they themselves possess the truth of their faith, and so they self-confidently and proudly endeavor to transmit it to the world, as if it did not emanate from Almighty God.

Yet, strange as it may seem, the Christian faith is the true religion, asserts Barth. That is to say, the revelation of God, the antithesis of *human* religion, is actually the true religion. It is true precisely because it eradicates all human religion. It is true in that through revelation man knows that his religion is only a human vanity, that there is really nothing for him to do but to repent and give thanks. It is true by virtue of its power to reconcile man with God, by virtue of its proclamation that all life and salvation come only through the grace of God. Christianity is true religion in that, through Christ, God justifies man. In the same manner, it can be said that by the grace of God the Christian Church and the children of God are the bearers of the true religion. And *by the grace of God* must be underlined. The Church and all who call themselves Christians must beware lest they arrogantly claim that through their merit they have become heir to the true faith. "They are what they are," Barth writes, "and their religion is the true religion, not because they recognize Him as such [i.e., as the Gracious God] and act accordingly, not in virtue of their religion of grace, but in virtue of the fact that God has graciously intervened for them, in virtue of His mercy in spite of their apparent but equivocal religion of grace, in virtue of the good pleasure which He has in them, in virtue of His free election, of which

[128]

this good pleasure is the only motive, in virtue of the Holy Spirit whom He willed to pour out upon them." [46] The Christian faith is true religion only through Jesus Christ.

In viewing the Christian faith as true religion, at least four facts should be kept in mind. First, Jesus Christ is the creator of the Christian religion, so that its reality rests solely in the name of Jesus Christ, and in no way is it brought into existence by man. To speak of the Christian religion apart from Jesus Christ is to succumb to the "liberal" heresy that the Christian religion is a possibility inherent within human nature. There can be no Christianity without Christ—i.e., the Christ who is "very God and Man." If Christ is for one moment ignored as the substance of Christianity, nothing remains. The Christian religion was and is and shall be only by virtue of the work of Jesus Christ.

Secondly, the Christian religion must be accounted for in terms of divine election, which is to say that it exists for no other reason than that it pleased God to make himself known through Jesus Christ. Had God not elected to reveal himself through Jesus Christ, the Christian religion simply would not be. God and God alone brought into being the covenant with the Hebrew people and later the fulfillment of the covenant through Jesus Christ. Man himself had absolutely nothing to do with the establishment of the Christian religion; it is a religion which is neither conceived nor sustained by human powers.

Thirdly, the truth of the Christian religion involves the act of divine justification or forgiveness of sins. This is implicit in the idea of election but should be made explicit. The story of the Church and of all Christians is one of unbelief; Christianity, like Buddhism or Islam, is unmistakably sinful, without justification. Only through the chastening and charity of God does the Christian religion become the true religion. It is only as God justifies it, as he justifies all sinners, that the Christian religion is absolutely different from all other religions. Humanly speaking, one can conclude that the acquittal of the Christian religion by God is inconceivable since Christianity is no more virtuous than all other religions. Thus, the question "Why has God's forgiveness been made known at this point and not at others?" Divine forgiveness is free and inscrutable, and it is quite in order for God to forgive where he chooses to forgive. It is sheer nonsense to juggle the possibilities of how God might have acted differently. The fact is that while all religions stand in need of God's justification, this condition has been granted *only* to the Christian religion.

Fourthly, the Christian religion, by virtue of its creation, election, and justification, is also involved in sanctification. Its responsibility is to proclaim the gospel to the end that by the grace of God man may be reconciled. It speaks the name of Jesus Christ, the very name by which it itself is justified. Although unfit to contain the power of God, it attests to that power; although incapable of holding the truth, it points to the truth; although unable to be holy, it extols the holy. The Christian religion, in its pointing and proclaiming, "can never have or claim any power or authority of its own. It will speak or be silent, work or rest, be known or not known, in virtue of the power and authority of the name of Jesus, effectual in the outpouring of the Holy Spirit." [47]

Karl Barth's stand regarding the relationship of the Christian faith to religion is unequivocally clear. Before the judgment of God, religion is not simply bad, it is totally perverse. It is the incarnation of human infidelity and the epitome of self-righteousness; it must be demolished. Barth is issuing a clarion call to all Christians to recognize the ultimate authority of revelation and the sinfulness of all religion. He is insisting that "we must learn again to understand revelation as *grace* and grace as *revelation*." It is tragic, says Barth, that the Protestant Church has succumbed to the seductions of religion, and contemporary theology has lost its content. The Christians have sold their birthright for a mess of religion—a transaction which represents the real catastrophe of modern Protestant theology. The law of God has been replaced by moral and sentimental maxims; Jesus Christ is now conceived to be the good man from Nazareth; the word of God has been absorbed by the word of man. The apologists for the faith have been so obsessed with reconciling Christianity to the spirit of the day that the unique, sovereign dimension of the gospel has disappeared. Christianity has become nothing more than the highest expression of man's religious instinct.

CHAPTER 6 The Christian Faith as the Judgment Against and the Fulfillment of Religion: Reinhold Niebuhr

REINHOLD NIEBUHR *was born in Wright City, Missouri, in June, 1892, the son of Gustav Niebuhr. His father, a German Evangelical pastor and a highly cultured person with a theologically sophisticated mind, was "the first formative religious influence" on Reinhold's life. It was through his father that he, along with his brother and sister, became familiar with the thought of some of Germany's outstanding theologians, particularly of Adolf von Harnack. In regard to his formal education, Niebuhr was educated first at the college and seminary of his denomination, Elmhurst College and Eden Theological Seminary, and later at the Divinity School of Yale University. He had gone to Yale with the intention of earning a doctor's degree in theology, but his impatience and boredom with the irrelevant probings into epistemology prompted him to foreswear graduate study and his plans for an academic career. Thus, in 1915, he departed from Yale without his degree (he acquired a score or more of*

*honorary degrees later) and, upon the order of his denomina-
tion, became pastor of the Bethel Evangelical Church in Detroit. Like Karl Barth, he found that his experience as a parish
minister helped to convince him that liberalism is too rosy and
glib to speak with any real relevance to the tragic and self-
contradictory character of human existence. Consequently, in
his search for a more forceful and cogent theology, he embarked on a re-examination of Biblical faith, a venture which
resulted in a decided shift in his theological emphasis. Upon
completing fifteen years as a parish minister, in 1928 Niebuhr
accepted the invitation to become professor of Applied Christian Ethics at Union Theological Seminary in New York City,
a position that he holds at the present time. While at Union
he has written no less than a dozen books, of which some of
the most well-known and provocative are* MORAL MAN AND
IMMORAL SOCIETY *(1932),* AN INTERPRETATION OF CHRISTIAN
ETHICS *(1935),* BEYOND TRAGEDY *(1937) and* THE NATURE AND
DESTINY OF MAN *(1941). His writings, along with his prophetic
voice as a preacher, have been among the chief influences that
have helped change the theological tide of America from liberalism to a "neo-orthodoxy."*

REINHOLD NIEBUHR stands somewhere between the Scylla
of Schleiermacher and the Charybdis of Barth. He agrees with
both men that religion, as the search for the ultimate meaning
of life, is a universal phenomenon; every man searches for purpose and seeks the final reason for his existence. But Niebuhr
quarrels with both Barth and Schleiermacher regarding the
nature of the Christian faith and its relation to religion. It is

not a matter of either "judgment" or "fulfillment," says Niebuhr; it is both of these. Faith censures all religion because the latter is invariably tainted with human pride and pretentiousness. In his religious strivings man always claims more virtue and knowledge than he actually possesses. Yet, the element of judgment notwithstanding, the human struggles and hopes contained within man's religion are ultimately fulfilled in the Christian faith. The incompleteness of religion is finally completed in the love of God in Christ.

Niebuhr's theology reflects myriad influences, including the great traditions of Western man. He has a knowledge of the life and thought of the Christian Church, as well as an understanding of the historical developments of the political, social, and economic life of the Western world. And, in one way or another, all of these schools and movements have left an imprint upon his thought. Nevertheless, notwithstanding the many traditions which have contributed to his thought, it is evident that, in the main, Niebuhr's theology moves back and forth between two poles: the spirit of the Enlightenment—the parent of liberal theology and the social gospel—and the historic affirmations of the Christian Church. It is largely in terms of the juxtaposition of these two movements that Niebuhr sets forth his highly dialectical and richly penetrating theology of the Christian faith.

The Enlightenment, Niebuhr explains, is primarily a testimony to the glory of man and to the conviction that it is through the singular use of human power and intelligence that the enigma of man's existence can be steadily and, in time, completely resolved. It is an expression of confidence in human nature and an affirmation that the future will bring about the strengthening and refining of man's moral fiber, until, at last, the bliss of paradise shall become a reality. It was this high idealism of the Enlightenment, Niebuhr goes on to say, which helped give birth to the Protestant liberalism and the social gospel. Like the proponents of the Age of Reason, says Niebuhr, the advocates of Protestant liberalism are certain that the heart of man is unblighted and that eventually the good will triumph. For the most part, they agree with the enlightened rationalists that there is nothing wrong with man that a good dose of sound education and moral discipline will not cure, and that, granted the purification of man's thoughts and the realignment of his loyalties, there is no reason why the world will not progressively move toward a state of perfection. Both cultural and religious liberals look with scorn upon many of the historical Christian affirmations, especially the traditional doctrines of the Trinity, the Divinity of Christ, and original sin. Thomas Jefferson is speaking not only for the Age of Reason, says Niebuhr, but for the liberal theologians as well when he repudiates the idea of the Trinity and goes on to assert that when "we shall have un-learned everything which has been taught since his [Jesus's] day and go back to the pure and simple doctrines which he inculcated, we shall then be truly and worthily his disciples and my opinion is if nothing has been added to what flowed purely from his lips, the whole world would all this day be Christian." [1] Indeed, Jefferson might well have proclaimed this from the Christian pulpit, for, says Niebuhr, "it is the naive optimism of the Age of Reason, rather than the more paradoxi-cal combination of pessimism and optimism of prophetic reli-gion, which the modern Church has preached as 'the simple gospel of Jesus.'" [2] Niebuhr's point is that cultural and religious

liberalism, both offspring of the Enlightenment, can be regarded as fraternal, if not identical, twins.

Niebuhr's early theological study and church work coin-
cided in time with the heyday of liberalism in America. It was
a time when the new theology and the social gospel were receiving a warm and extensive approbation, and Niebuhr was
not inclined to divorce himself from these movements. He
encountered the tenets of liberalism long before he pursued
his formal education at college and seminary. Early in his
life he became acquainted with the thought of some of
Germany's eminent theologians, particularly of Adolf von Harnack. Harnack is heir to the liberal tradition inaugurated by
Schleiermacher and Ritschl, and is himself, in no small measure,
instrumental in spreading the gospel of liberalism to the inner-
most and outermost parts of the Protestant world. Harnack
contends that the doctrinal and ecclesiastical accretions of the
gospel must be immediately cast off so that the simple message
of Jesus may be proclaimed in all of its unmistakable clarity.
St. Paul's exposition of the faith must be disclaimed and the
idea of miracles must be repudiated, says Harnack. The true
meaning of the faith is contained in the gospels, for they "offer
us a plain picture of Jesus' teaching," of his vocation, and of
the "impression which he made upon his disciples." Harnack
finds that the real genius of the Christian faith is made known
in the "historical Jesus," rather than in the "Christ of Faith."
In this connection he insists that *The Gospel, as Jesus proclaimed it, has to do with the Father only and not with the
Son.*" [3] In other words, Jesus is not *in* the gospel, as a part of the
message, but is rather the *personal realization* and *power* of the
gospel. Christ is not the one who discloses the ultimate will of

God; He is one who has an unusual knowledge of God and His gospel, and He "was its personal realization and its strength." There is no need for dogmatic and labyrinthine formulations concerning the significance of Jesus, says Harnack; everything which Jesus intended to teach can be reduced to three basic ideas:

> Firstly, the kingdom of God and its coming.
> Secondly, God the Father and the infinite value of the human soul.
> Thirdly, the higher righteousness and the commandment of love.[4]

Running through Harnack's version of the gospel is the idea that the Kingdom of God, as an ethical phenomenon, is at the heart of the Christian faith, and that Jesus, the central figure of Christianity, epitomizes a Godly way of life which does not exceed the potential goodness found within man. For Harnack, the infinite God is infinitely short of being the "totally Other."

But, granted Niebuhr's familiarity with Harnack's thought, the influence which was greater on Neibuhr than that of any one person from across the Atlantic was the strong liberal spirit in America. During the three decades preceding 1920, many erudite persons throughout the country made it known that they would not subscribe to the tenets of orthodox Christianity. In order to be in the swim of things one had to be a liberal. For example, how could an intelligent person, it was argued, subscribe to the foolish affirmation of the Apostles' Creed: "I believe in the forgiveness of sins, the resurrection of the body and the life everlasting"? This article of faith and many others were roundly disclaimed. Orthodoxy was treated with condescension, while liberalism was welcomed in the best religious circles.

Within both ecclesiastical and academic communities, persons who desired a sophisticated theology found the social gospel and its underlying presuppositions to be intellectually satisfying. They sought to modernize the gospel, extolling the merits of a theology which was in harmony with the contemporary scientific and philosophical thought and beckoning everyone to join in so employing the resources of religion that the Kingdom of God may come on earth.

Chief among the American proponents of the social gospel is Walter Rauschenbusch. Rauschenbusch believes that the central theme of the gospel is the Kingdom of God: "The Kingdom of God contains the theology of the Christian religion." For Rauschenbusch the term *Kingdom* does not mean an eschatological reality but an historical hope. The Kingdom of God "must be done on earth, as it is done in heaven." It is "the establishment of a community of righteousness in mankind"; it is "the energy of God realizing itself in human life"; it is "humanity organized according to the Will of God"; it is "the Christian transfiguration of the social order." [5] Rauschenbusch, relying upon the liberal theology of the Continent and imbued with the secular progressivism of America, endeavors to convince the people that God is once again at work in the world. Notwithstanding his somewhat restrained hopes for the future, he does not believe it imprudent for men to look forward to the "great day" ahead. The expression "restrained hopes" must not be overlooked. Unlike several other prophets of the social gospel, Rauschenbusch is never so naive as to believe that the sin of man can be entirely eradicated. At the same time, in keeping with the utopian motif of the social gospel, he does not hesitate to assert that the Kingdom of God "implies a progressive reign of love in human affairs." The future holds bright promises. To the question: What is the task of the Christian preacher? Rauschenbusch gives a clear answer: The conscience of the Christian must be quickened to mankind's social evils so that society may be duly Christianized: cooperation, equality, collective property rights, and democracy—instead of competition, autocracy, monopoly, privilege, and capitalism.

It is within the theological climate of this relatively simple and extraordinarily optimistic faith of the social gospel that Niebuhr embarked upon his theological career. But his benign gospel was soon challenged. His experience as a parish minister helped to convince him of the frailty of liberalism. What specifically caused him to change his mind? It was the social and economic revolution which was taking place right before his eyes in Detroit. Henry Ford's industrial enterprise was rapidly expanding, making Detroit the country's automobile capital. In the midst of this aggrandizement of power and wealth, Niebuhr was prompted to question the moral pretensions of Mr. Ford who, because of his famous five-dollar-a-day wage, was widely lauded as a benevolent entrepreneur. Niebuhr observed firsthand that the idealism for which Ford was acclaimed was in fact permeated by the corruptions of self-interest, bringing hardship and suffering to those who were victims of Ford's policies. Thus it was through his duties as a parish minister—rather than the international crisis or academic study—that Niebuhr discovered that "the simple idealism into which the classical faith had evaporated was as irrelevant to the crises of personal life as it was to the complex social issues of an industrial city." [6]

[140]

Having realized the inanity of liberalism, Niebuhr proceeded to search for a more cogent and forceful delineation of the Christian faith. And among the many persons who helped to guide him on his new theological venture, St. Augustine and Kierkegaard are not among the least of them. St. Augustine— in retrospect, Niebuhr is amazed that he was so late in carefully studying this Latin Church father—revealed to Niebuhr, perhaps more than any other theologian, the fallacy of identifying moral idealism of the social gospel with the Christian faith. The righteousness of God is radically different from the righteousness of man, says Augustine. Man, in his sinfulness, separates himself from God so that the ways of man are always unlike the ways of God. And the sin of man is pride: man desires to be God rather than man, therein "forsaking Him to whom the soul ought solely to cleave, as the beginning thereof, to make the self seem the beginning." [7] This belief, that sin is pride, casts its shadow upon virtually every book which Niebuhr has written. It is the pivotal idea around which his entire "neo-orthodox" theology revolves. At the same time, while St. Augustine believes that man is separated from God, he is also certain that man always retains an affinity for God. Made in the image of God, man is forever stirred to find the God to whom he belongs; he is restless until he has found Him. Niebuhr finds Augustine's idea of the image of God in man to be exceedingly instructive. It is, says Niebuhr, the most convincing statement regarding the "relevance and distance between the human and the divine." And, continues Niebuhr, "all the subsequent statements on the image of God in man [and, one might add, especially the statement of Niebuhr himself] are indebted to Augustine."

[141]

Niebuhr's theological lineage can also be traced to Kierkegaard. The Danish prophet portrayed the Christian message as essentially a "paradox," totally inexplicable within the boundaries of human reason. Beneath all the verities of faith is the revelation of God in Jesus Christ, forever a riddle and offense to the human mind. Kierkegaard, as Niebuhr interprets him, provides a most trenchant rebuttal to all theological liberalism. Alongside of Kierkegaard's insistence upon the paradox of faith, the moral idealism of liberalism appears insipid. Echoing Kierkegaard's claim that faith can never be reduced to a rational system, Niebuhr insists that the Christian faith is perforce "foolishness to the Greeks." Again, Kierkegaard, contrary to the spirit of Protestant liberalism, emphasizes the sinfulness of man. Like St. Augustine, he contends that sin is essentially pride. For Kierkegaard the opposite of sin is not goodness, but faith—i.e., sin is faithlessness, or the trusting of oneself instead of God. Niebuhr, as already indicated, finds the idea of sin as pride to be far more congruous with both Biblical faith and the realities of human existence than is liberalism's moralistic account of sin. Thus it is that Kierkegaard and Augustine were among those persons who helped Niebuhr gain an appreciation of some of the central doctrines of classical Christianity. Perhaps more than anything else, they helped Niebuhr see the truth in the Christine affirmation that God is radically different from man, and that equating the human with the divine—as liberalism tends to do—is sheer idolatry.

Niebuhr is a theologian who takes seriously both the "temper of modernity" and the "fundamental faith." Unlike many of his distinguished predecessors, as well as contemporaries, he refuses to retreat to either one of these positions; both must be

taken seriously. But the question arises: "Can two walk together, except they be agreed?" (to quote Amos out of context).
Niebuhr answers Yes and No. And this double answer reveals
the dialectical thrust of Niebuhr's theology. How is it true that
modern thought and the Christian faith *do* and *do not* walk
together? Modern liberal thought is not without its measure of
truth, says Niebuhr. For is it not clearly evident that the liberals
are the instruments of ultimate truth when they denounce a
sterile, orthodox Christianity which has transmuted "a religion
of love into a support of traditional and historic injustice"?
The modern minds, he says, are obviously right when they
assign "an immediate reverence for politics and economics to
the law of love and the ideal of brotherhood." In other words,
the liberals, in holding high the law of love, recapture an essential element of prophetic religion which traditional Christianity
is strongly prone to disregard. Moreover, says Niebuhr, it must
not be denied that the modern historical research and scientific
reason have helped emancipate man from crude superstition
and authoritarian powers. The enlightened reason has contributed to man's freedom. It has played a significant part in
helping men to understand the universe and to discover the
worth of human personality. And, warns Niebuhr, the Christian
theologian, as he sets forth his theological understanding of
the Christian faith, dare not fail to respect liberalism's contribution to truth.

At the same time, says Niebuhr, the historic faith of the
Church reminds us that liberalism is grossly in error—it fails
to recognize the depth of man's evil. In its naive optimism,
liberalism tries to laugh out of court the traditional Christian
doctrine of the sinful pride of man. In its simple and sentimental

idealism the realities of life are obscured and the corruption of man's self-interest are treated too lightly. Niebuhr insists that the traditional Christian appraisal of man is far more realistic than is the one offered by liberalism—after all, man *is* a sinful creature. All men stand under the judgment of God, for all human action and thought are tainted with an inordinate self-love. Every man thinks more highly of himself than he ought to think. In other words, the distance between God and man is far greater than the liberals believe.

This discussion of the historical orientation of Niebuhr's thought has been brief but, nevertheless, instructive. Through it we see that it is Niebuhr's insistence that both modern thought and the Christian tradition be taken seriously. This provides us with a clue for understanding his theology. It is within the matrix of this dialectical tension that his theology takes form— and that he sets forth the idea that the Christian faith is both the judgment against and the fulfillment of religion.

Niebuhr is convinced that religion is a phenomenon common to all mankind, that it is part of man's original relatedness to God. He contends that every person, by virtue of his existence as a human being, is also a religious being. The common practice of attributing religion to one person and denying it to another is indefensible. Neither can one refer to one period of history as religious and to another as nonreligious, for no era of mankind has been without religion. Thus, for Niebuhr, the prevailing tendency to refer to the contemporary religious mood in America as a renaissance of religion is totally erroneous. While it may be true that from the viewpoint of historic Christianity the present crisis of mankind may be more religiously propitious, the fact remains that the twentieth century is no

[144]

more religious than the preceding ones. Religion is not a phenomenon of a particular historical situation or era but of mankind as such.[8]

The predominant drive of religion, according to Niebuhr, is the inexorable desire to find meaning for life. Religion is preoccupied with the "whence" and the final "wherefore" of human existence. Man is so created that he cannot be indifferent to the perils of his life or inattentive to the nature of his destiny. Why am I here and where am I going? This is man's perennial concern. He wants to know whether there is any sense to all the nonsense of life and whether there is a unified and coherent meaning by which the human soul can be sustained. But, a skeptical voice inquires, are *all* men possessed by this desire to find a meaning? What about the cynic who disavows any real meaning for life, who seemingly is uninvolved and is concerned only about detailed facts? Is he not an exception? Niebuhr's answer is that the cynic, too, constructs some sort of cosmic and meaningful system from which he derives the purpose and direction of his life. Although the cynic's answer may differ from the theist's, he still shares with all men a longing for meaning.

In some of his later works—especially his *The Nature and Destiny of Man*—Niebuhr accounts for the genesis of religion in terms of "general revelation." What this phrase means is that, among other things, by virtue of man's relatedness to God no man is ever totally without some awareness, dim and veiled though it may be, of the Eternal and that this awareness is part of man's endowment as a creature of God. The religiousness of man signifies that God himself has instilled within the human spirit a longing for that which transcends the human spirit.

More specifically, Niebuhr explains, the concept of "general revelation" connotes three ideas concerning man's relatedness to God: "the sense of reverence for a majesty and of dependence upon an ultimate source of being," "the sense of moral obligation laid upon one from beyond oneself and of moral unworthiness before a judge," and "the longing for forgiveness." [9] It should be noted that "general revelation" is a view which Niebuhr and Emil Brunner hold in common. Brunner calls it "original revelation" instead of "general revelation" but, semantics notwithstanding, he shares with Niebuhr the idea that behind all religion lies the testimony of God to himself. "Apart from real revelation," Brunner writes, "the phenomenon of religion cannot be understood. Even the most primitive polytheistic or prepolytheistic idolatrous religion is unintelligible without the presupposition of the universal revelation of God which has been given to all men through the Creation." [10]

The universal phenomenon of religion is expressed according to two main types, says Niebuhr. One type includes the "primitive" and "ultra-modern" religion and is characterized by its lack of depth. It does not probe very deeply into the plight of man; it is inclined to resolve the enigma of human existence too quickly and too easily. Rather than constantly inquiring and endeavoring to reckon with the total dimensions of life, it shrinks the human world so that it becomes manageable. In the case of primitive religion it is satisfied with a *limited* cosmos: it finds meaning through loyalty to a tribe or through the worship of some natural object. And in modern religion, it settles for a *superficial* cosmos: it believes that the naturalistic and humanistic movements—e.g., humanism, moralism, naturalism, materialism—contain the efficacy of meaning.

The other main type of religion, which Niebuhr calls "high" religion, is distinguished by its quality of depth. It takes man's entire existence seriously. The tragic and fragmentary character of life is solemnly encountered; the incoherence and disunity of human knowledge is candidly admitted; the impotent and corrupt nature of mortal man is openly confronted. There is no covering up. With deep apprehension but obstinate honesty, man and his world are acknowledged for what they are.

The virtue of high religion lies in its superior capacity to point to the transcendent dimension of life. Through its courageous and extensive explorations of human existence there comes the suggestion of that which transcends human existence. Depth bears the forewarnings of God. The deeper the probing the more impressive becomes the fact that the vastness and the complexity and the incongruity of life can gain meaning, not through human reason, but through a reality which is itself higher and greater than man's enigmatic existence. In the struggle for meaning it becomes apparent that "the forms of life are too various and multifarious to be ascribed easily to a single source or related to a single realm of meaning if the source does not transcend all the observable facts and forces." [11] Through depth there is the pointing to a "transcendent source of meaning by which alone confidence in the meaningfulness of life and existence can be maintained." [12]

At this point a brief digression is necessary. During the time of Niebuhr's early writings he frequently used the term "religion" as being synonymous with the "Christian faith." These terms were used interchangeably because at this stage of his thinking he carried strong vestiges of liberalism and, thus, still asserted that Christianity is—as Professor Hans Hoffman explains—only a peculiar manifestation of universal religiousness.[13] Niebuhr's explanation, given above, of the two types of religion is taken from his *Christian Ethics,* written in 1935. Yet, even at this time he still did not make a clear distinction between religion and the Christian faith. Thus, it should be kept in mind that the phrase "high religion," found in his *Christian Ethics,* actually embraces the Christian faith. It is only as his thought develops further that his writings reflect the clear differentiation between the Christian faith on the one hand and religion on the other, and that he ceases to employ the two terms interchangeably. And it is, of course, with this later period that this study is primarily concerned.[14]

What then, according to Niebuhr, is the relation of the Christian faith to religion? Christianity's vantage point for viewing religion is Jesus Christ; He is the final word on all life, the word beyond which there is no other word. Jesus Christ reveals *the* truth, *the ultimate* meaning. Through Christ's life and death, God's crowning testimony has been given; God has disclosed Himself. For a long time man had been expecting God to make Himself known, the most dramatic expression of this expectation being the Messianism of the Old Testament. At last this hope was fulfilled—in Jesus Christ the power and glory of God were made known. Niebuhr declares that "in the life, death and resurrection of Christ, the expected disclosure of God's sovereignty over history, and the expected establishment of that sovereignty had taken place." [15]

Through Christ, man knows that the ultimate truth of life is love. "The good news of the gospel," writes Niebuhr, "is that God takes the sinfulness of man into Himself; and overcomes in His own heart what cannot be overcome in human life." [16] This is the transcendent meaning—in Christ, God reconciles man to Himself, and nothing can separate man from the love which is in Christ. God is love. It is true that God condemns all man's sinfulness; His judgment against man must never be forgotten. Niebuhr recalls the words of St. Paul: "For the wrath of God is revealed from heaven against all ungodliness and unrighteousness of men, who hold the truth in unrighteousness." [17] In the name of God, all man's ignoble motives and iniquitous acts must be denounced. Yet, the "Christian Faith sees in the Cross of Christ the assurance that judgment is not the final word of God to man." [18] The final word is that God's love and redemption transcend His judgment. Jesus Christ "is recognized by the eyes of faith as the point where the heavens are opened and the divine mystery is disclosed and the love of God toward man shines down upon him; and man is no longer afraid, even though he knows himself to be involved in the crucifixion." [19] In love, the God who transcends all history enters the human scene and, by identifying Himself with man's guilt, redeems him. "God speaks to man in the Incarnation; and the content of the revelation is an act of reconciliation in which the judgment of God upon the pride of man is not abrogated. . . . Nevertheless the final word is not one of judgment but of mercy and forgiveness." [20] The love of God is great enough to overcome all sin.

Jesus Christ, the bearer of the good news of love, is not a man but a God-man, Niebuhr declares. That is, He is human but is at the same time divine; He is both fully human and fully divine. And strange as it may seem, the reality of the one dimension of His life does not diminish the reality of the other: ". . . he is not less divine for being human and temporal and not less human and temporal for being fully divine." [21] God-man is a way of affirming that the word became flesh, an affirmation which embraces the whole character of the Christian faith. "It asserts," writes Niebuhr, "that God's word is relevant to human life. It declares that an event in history can be of such a character as to reveal the character of history itself." [22] It asserts that apart from Jesus Christ the ultimate meaning of human existence cannot be known.

Niebuhr seeks to restore to modern theology a Biblical Christology. The Christian affirmation, he proclaims, is that Jesus Christ is unique, bringing to the human realm that which transcends human experience. "The truth which is revealed in the Cross," he states, "is not a truth which could have been anticipated in human culture and it is not the culmination of human wisdom." [23] This does not mean—as will become evident later—that Christ "stands perpetually in contradiction to experience." Yet, it does mean that the truth and love of Jesus Christ is ultimately given to man by God and that it is not derived from the human mind, not even by the most enlightened and righteous mind. In Jesus Christ alone is the final word of God made known—the final word on all life, on all religion.

Niebuhr finds the liberals' view of Christ to be untenable; as he sees it the liberals have denied Christ's true nature. They have rejected the orthodox Christology, asserting that it is an offense to the integrity of the sophisticated mind. They have insisted that Christ must be portrayed in a manner compatible with the most recent philosophical and scientific knowledge and within the boundaries of human reason. And what this position means, Niebuhr concludes, is that Jesus Christ is conceived to be a good man, a bright and shining example for all men to emulate. The liberals have imagined Jesus Christ to be another great—perhaps the greatest—historical figure. Thus, Christ is denied His transcendent status. He becomes the highest example, the wise teacher and courageous prophet, and *so long* as no one surpasses His excellence He merits man's allegiance. In Niebuhr's words, the liberals affirm "that Jesus was a very, very, very good man but that of course a better man might appear, at a future date, in which case the loyalty of the faithful would be transferred to him." [24] (And in expressing this disapprobation of the liberal view, Niebuhr has not resorted to caricature. It was Schleiermacher who, at one time, explained: "Hereafter there will be more, for the whole being of man is not yet by any means embodied in the peculiar form of Christianity, but, despite what is said of its speed, its already accomplished overthrow, Christianity will yet have a long history." [25]) In their repudiation of the orthodox doctrine, says Niebuhr, "the Christ of orthodox faith is transmuted into the 'historic Jesus' who 'incarnates values worthy of our highest devotion.'" [26]

With Jesus Christ as its vantage point, Niebuhr declares, the Christian faith issues a No against religion. This condemnatory pronouncement arises from the fact that all religion is subject to the corruption of sin: it is always more or less a glorification of the self. Emil Brunner, whose position on this entire subject parallels Niebuhr's, recalls St. Paul's words: "Because that, knowing God, they glorified Him not as God

. . . but became vain in their reasonings . . . and changed the glory of the incorruptible God for the likeness of an image of corruptible man, and of birds, and four-footed beasts, and creeping things." [27] For Niebuhr, too, the religious man deifies himself and his world; he rebels against God and strives to take on the prerogatives and duties of the Almighty.

Viewed in a larger perspective, the theology of Niebuhr explains that the blemish of all religion can be accounted for in this way. Man is a creature of God, and the meaning of his life is derived through his relationship to his Creator. As a creature, his life bears two dimensions. On the one hand, like the animal he is identified with the world of nature. He cannot escape the necessity for eating, sleeping, and satisfying certain psychological needs. He is forever conditioned by the physical world and by the processes of nature. On the other hand, man also transcends all nature; unlike all other animals he is spirit; i.e., he is a self-conscious being. He possesses the unique capacity to stand off and look at himself. "Man is the only mortal animal," Niebuhr writes, "who knows that he is mortal, a fact which proves that in some sense he is not mortal. Man is the only creature imbedded in the flux of finitude who knows that this is his fate, which proves that in some sense this is not his fate." [28] He is endowed with the freedom to choose between good and evil, truth and falsity, the beautiful and the ugly.

But, continues Niebuhr's explanation, man rebels against his "creatureliness"—i.e., the dual dimensional nature of his life. The two natures, standing in juxtaposition to each other, are more than man can bear, and he becomes tense, frustrated, and desperate; being a creature of both nature and spirit, of necessity and freedom, man becomes anxious. What is his way out of this plight? He chooses to quell his anxiety by resolving his predicament *prematurely*. And herein lies his sin. He sins in that he disclaims the fact that his creaturely being can find meaning only as it is identified with its Creator. He disclaims this fact by taking his life into his own hands. He tries to manage his life by denying the contingent character of his existence and by escaping from his freedom. Unwilling to let God control his life he attempts to control it himself. He trusts himself. He presumes that he is self-contained and that "man is the measure of all things." In this way he overreaches the limits of his creatureliness. In theological language he is guilty of the sin of pride. He arrogantly pre-empts the prerogatives that belong to God. Niebuhr is puzzled by the fact that modern man has attached a primitive stigma to the idea of a jealous God. "God is necessarily jealous," says Niebuhr, "because the root of man's sin lies in his pretension of being God." He then goes on to explain that the corruption of man is not due simply to man's shortsightedness or ignorance; the real trouble is that "men are tempted to protest against their finiteness by seeking to make themselves infinite. . . . The devil is always an angel who pretends to be God." [29]

Thus it is that man's religion is always tainted with the hue of self-love. The idols of the self are held up for veneration, and man falls down to worship them. In religion the self is deified. The wisdom of man is elevated to too lofty a height and the goodness of man is set on too high a pinnacle; the human and contingent are raised to an absolute and unlimited dimension. The religious man thinks more highly of himself than he ought to think; he seeks his own salvation and is preeminently bent on gaining security. The fact is that the life of man is potentially most demonic precisely at the point where it takes on a religious dimension. Brunner expresses the viewpoint in this way: "The original sin of man breaks out first of all, and mainly, in his religion: the essence of original sin is man's apostasy and his inveterate tendency to be absorbed in himself." [30] Nothing is as sinful as man's religious sin. There are, according to Niebuhr, four types of sinful pride:

the pride of "power," which is man's unwillingness to recognize the contingent and dependent nature of his life and to grasp for power to make himself secure;

the pride of "intellect," which designates the human disposition to ignore the ideological taint of all human knowledge and to pretend that man's knowledge is a statement of ultimate truth;

"moral" pride, which refers to man's unwillingness to recognize his sinfulness and to ascribe final righteousness to his relative moral standards;

and "spiritual" pride, which constitutes man's worst sin.

"The ultimate sin," says Niebuhr, "is the religious sin of making the self-deification implied in moral pride explicit. This is done when our partial standards and relative attainments are explicitly related to the unconditioned good, and claim divine sanction. For this reason religion is not simply as is generally supposed an inherently virtuous human quest for God. It is merely a final battleground between God and man's self-esteem. In that battle even the most pious practices may be instruments of human pride." [31] Jesus's most scathing judgments, says Niebuhr, were directed against the very religious Pharisees, who, in their self-righteousness assumed the virtues and prerogatives of God. For in the claim that they were more righteous than others, the Pharisees were guilty of the worst form of sin. Niebuhr finds himself in complete agreement with Hendrik Kraemer's statement: "What goes by the name of 'religion' in the modern world is to a great extent unbridled human self-assertion in religious disguise." [32]

Thus, in the sin of pride, religion gives rise to the most uncharitable and ruthless kind of human conduct. In the religious man's self-deification he becomes unqualifiedly confident of the virtue of his schemes and enterprises for the social order; convinced that his plans merit universal acclaim, he bumptiously decrees the order of things and haughtily appropriates the right to manipulate people as he pleases. "The worst form of class domination," writes Niebuhr, "is religious class domination in which, as for instance in the Indian caste system, a dominant priestly class not only subjects subordinate classes to social disabilities but finally excludes them from participation in any universe of meaning. The worst form of intolerance is religious intolerance, in which the particular interests of the contestants hide behind religious absolutes. The worst form of self-assertion is religious self-assertion in which under the guise of contrition before God, He is claimed as the exclusive ally of our contingent self." [33] In the name of religion men claim the right of eminent domain, and ruthlessly shove aside anyone who comes in their way. Seemingly, Niebuhr heartily concurs with Herbert Butterfield: "It is even possible that the great wars should come about because idealists are too egotistical concerning their own plans of salvation for mankind, and because the righteous are stiff-necked." [34]

Thus far, one thing is clear: The Christian faith stands in judgment against all religion. At the same time, Niebuhr is equally certain that the Christian faith is also the fulfillment of religion; there is not only a No but also a Yes. Barth, of course, depicted man to be so totally evil that any possibility of fulfillment is automatically ruled out. But Niebuhr is convinced that Barth has represented man as being far more iniquitous than he actually is and that, given a more realistic portrayal of man, the Christian faith rightly signifies fulfillment. By realistic portrayal Niebuhr means, among other things, that it simply is not true that man is totally depraved, without any capacity for the good. There is in man a goodness (along with the evil) which cannot be eradicated even by the most demonic expressions of sin. If man were entirely evil, how could he be held responsible for his life? How could a human being who has no more probity than a cat (as Barth claims in his debate with Brunner) be held accountable for his thoughts and actions? Niebuhr asserts that without the good the evil would be impossible; the good is possible without evil but evil is a parasite of the good. This is the universal testimony of human experience: disorder is possible only if there is order, and disease is possible only if there is health. So it is that man would know nothing of evil if he were totally without good. A man may be vile and destroy himself, but he does so only by availing himself of his goodness. St. Augustine, Niebuhr points out, expressed it in this way: "And it was manifested unto me that those things be good, which yet are corrupted; which neither were they sovereignly good nor unless they were good could be corrupted: for if sovereignly good, they were incorruptible, if not good at all there is nothing in them to be corrupted." [35]

On this point Niebuhr's theology must not be misconstrued. When he speaks of the goodness of man he (and Augustine, too, for that matter) is not granting man either the capacity to ascertain absolute truth or the ability to exemplify ultimate righteousness. Or, to express the point differently, he is not saying that man is empowered to give rise to the Christian faith. The gospel which is disclosed by Jesus Christ is radically different from what man in his religion can ever know. What Niebuhr is averring is this: because of a residual goodness within man, religion is a "point of contact" whereby God comes to man; the religious strivings of man, while they always fall short of God, nevertheless point toward God. In religion men seek two conditions: (a) they earnestly seek the truth—the truth from which they are removed, and (b) they seriously long for love— the love from which they are estranged. Truth and love—these are requirements which spring from the very nature of man; they are a part of the law of his being; they are at the heart of his religious struggle. And what Niebuhr is saying is that it is precisely through man's preoccupation with these two conditions that God comes to man. Look more closely at this matter.

Man searches for truth, and it is this inquiring spirit which distinguishes him as a religious creature. But the final truth which he seeks is always beyond his grasp. Man is both too ignorant and too sinful ever to ascertain ultimate knowledge. The last word on life, says Niebuhr, "is not something which simple men believe upon authority and wiser men deduce from experience." There is in ultimate truth something "which defies the wisdom of both wise and foolish, more particularly of the wise." [36] Yet, the fact is that the human mind is never so depraved that it is precluded from contributing to man's quest for meaning. The human mind is not without merit for the very reason that it always contains the power to point to the incapacity of the mind itself to discover the truth. Even in its sinfulness it is "sufficiently free to transcend itself and to know something of its own finiteness." [37] According to Niebuhr, "Neither the finiteness of the human mind nor the sinful corruption of the mind or the 'ideological taint' in all human culture can completely efface the human capacity for the apprehension of the true wisdom. Since there can be no total corruption of truth or virtue there is always a residual desire for the true wisdom, and the real God and the final revelation of the meaning of life, below and above the sinful tendency to build a world of meaning around ourselves as the center." [38] Thus it is that through the human search for truth, blind and stammering though it may be, God's grace comes to man.

And if the subject is shifted from "truth" to "love," the principal facts are not altered. Love is written within the heart of man, and it represents the fulfillment of man's life. The true self is realized when it is moved not by calculation but by "'grace' which draws the self out of itself despite itself into the love of God and the neighbor." [39] The presence of love means the realization of the self, and the absence of love "results in a narrower and more self-contained self." [40] Love is the authentic norm; it is the last, the highest norm. It stands over against all of man's lovelessness. Love is the content of the conscience which makes man uneasy about his life. It is because of the law of love that every effort to relegate all conduct as simply natural is betrayed by the frenzy of rationalization and a fidgety spirit. It is the criterion by which all things are reckoned. It is through love that the self is fulfilled. Now, while it is true that the human manifestation of love is always colored by the sin of pride and requires the grace of God to redeem it, it is no less true that the demands of the law of love and the consequent uneasy conscience is the "point of contact" wherein God's redemption of man occurs. It is in awareness of the violation of the law of love that divine grace is imparted. Thus, while human love always falls short of what it ought to be, it is also true that "faith in Christ could find no lodging place in the human soul, were it not uneasy about the contrast between its true and its present state." [41]

Translated into a more ethical context (remember that Niebuhr never failed to relate his theology to social, political, and economic situations) he is saying this: The love of the Kingdom of God is both the negation and the completion of historical justice. Love is the ultimate requirement which justice seeks to satisfy. Yet, every expression of justice is a contradiction of perfect love. In other words—in keeping with Niebuhr's entire theology—love and justice stand in a dialectical relation to each other. On the one hand, systems, rules, and laws of justice always violate the law of love. This is true because justice always embodies the sinful element that is inherent in all human existence—that attitude whereby man is concerned more about his own welfare than about the welfare of others. The very structures of justice betray the presence of man's self-interest. "The fence and the boundary line," writes Niebuhr, "are the symbols of the spirit of justice. They set the limits upon each man's interest to prevent one from taking advantage of the other." [42] Every man sees the world from his own limited perspective, and he invariably exaggerates his own importance beyond its true boundary. He can never be as impartial, as disinterested, as he ought to be. Thus he always infringes upon the rights and privileges of others. In this sense, the systems of justice always stand in a negative relation to love. On the other hand, the systems, rules, and laws which govern human relationships—i.e., justice—are the means through which the commandment of love is approximated. Justice is the servant of love; it provides the laws and structures whereby men in their social relations can realize the conditions of mutuality and community. Through justice men synthesize their differences and arrive at tolerable solutions to their problems. Thus it is that justice stands in a positive relation to love.

Niebuhr's viewpoint will become clearer if we see how he relates it to concrete situations. Consider, for example, the matter of unemployment. The privileged class inevitably insists, Niebuhr explains, that the benefits granted to the unfortunate class are more or less excessive. In fact, there are those among the economically well off who denounce all unemployment benefits on the ground that persons in such a destitute condition are slothful and therefore undeserving. Thus, the unemployment benefits stand in contradiction to the law of love. On the other hand, unemployment benefits are an expression of the concern of the more privileged for the less fortunate. These benefits are administered through agencies of the community which execute their responsibilities according to fixed principles. Thus, there is a positive relation between justice and the ultimate norm of love.

Consider another example: the nature of government.

Government always contains the "twin perils of tyranny and anarchy," two conditions which can never be completely obliterated from any political arrangement. And what these perils represent are "the sinful elements of conflict and dominion" which stand in "contradiction to the ideal of brotherhood on every level of communal organization." [43] Thus, even the highest form of government harbors elements which violate the final law of love. But it is no less true that the political system helps preserve order and freedom. Government provides powers which constrain evil and preserve human rights. And in providing these conditions, government makes possible a justice which points toward the law of love.

Niebuhr summarizes the relation of love and justice in this way: "The positive relation of principles of justice to the ideal of brotherhood makes an indeterminate approximation of love in the realm of justice possible. The negative relation means that all historic conceptions of justice will embody some elements which contradict the law of love. The interests of a class, the viewpoint of a nation, the prejudices of an age and the illusions of a culture are consciously and unconsciously insinuated into the norms by which men regulate their common life." [44]

Niebuhr's theology is complex and subtle, and efforts to treat any aspect of it in too simple and succinct a manner only yield serious distortion. Yet, it is evident that for Niebuhr the Christian faith is both judgment against and fulfillment of religion. The Christian faith does not simply stand in opposition to human experience, it is inherently related to human experience; it does not only remind man that he lives in darkness, it illuminates the darkness; it does not simply tell man of his meaningless existence, it gives meaning to the meaningless. The ultimate truth which the religious man seeks, but cannot find, is finally given in the Christian faith. "By completing the incompleteness, clarifying the obscurities and correcting the falsifications of human knowledge it [the Christian faith] becomes true wisdom to 'them that are called.'" [45]

CHAPTER 7 Conclusion

To this point no attempt has been made to evaluate the five positions that have been presented in this study. Although the author's bias has been showing at times, the chapters are intended to present a reasonably accurate report of what other persons have thought. But, having completed this more restrained task, perhaps it is now lawful and expedient to offer a critical appraisal of this material. Of course, any effort to issue a final verdict on the subject would be ludicrous. Matters of such a vast and complex nature defy an easy resolution. At the same time, perhaps it is not unreasonable to bring to the surface some of the undercurrents of the study and to suggest a vantage point from which the various positions may be duly assessed.

Throughout Biblical faith there are certain affirmations which are singularly decisive to our understanding of Christianity and which bear a peculiar relevance to our present inquiry concerning faith and religion. What I have in mind are the Biblical declarations regarding the *imago Dei*, the Incarnation, and the *eschaton*. Together these three central aspects of

Biblical faith provide us with a perspective for judging the relative merits of the several positions set forth earlier.

According to Genesis, the creative work of the Almighty includes the creation of man. "So God created man in his own image, in the image of God he created him." What is meant by the term *image*? It means that there is an affinity between God and man, that man is always striving to live in fellowship with God, that man is restless until he has found God. "Image of God" is the Biblical way of saying that man is concerned about the meaning of his existence. Man is so fashioned that he cannot be satisfied with his life. St. Augustine's wrestling with God may be somewhat unique in its intensity, but its essential nature is not unlike that found in other men: "I dive on this side and on that," Augustine writes, "as far as I can, and there is no end. So great is the force of memory, so great the force of life, even in the mortal life of man. What shall I do then, O Thou my true life, my God." [1] Within man there is an irrepressible longing to seek the fullness of his life, to know something of the true heights and depths of his existence. According to the book of Ecclesiasticus:

> The Lord created man of the earth . . .
> He endued them with strength proper to them;
> And made them according to his own image . . .
> He filled them with knowledge of wisdom,
> And shewed them good and evil.
> He set his eye upon their hearts,
> To shew them the majesty of his works. . . .
>
> (17:1 ff.)

Is not this passage an expression of man's "impulse to worship"? By virtue of the image which has been stamped upon him, man cannot be indifferent to his existence. Within him there persists an unrelenting desire to penetrate the final mystery of his life, to gain ultimate meaning and fulfillment.

It is true that the "image" in man is defaced—it is corrupted. According to the myth in Genesis about Adam and Eve, all human concerns are corrupted by the inordinate desire for power, by man's thinking more highly of himself than he ought to think. St. Paul, too, reminds us that man "exchanged the truth about God for a lie and worshipped and served the creature rather than the Creator" and that "all have sinned and fall short of the glory of God." At the same time, it is erroneous to conclude that man has been so corrupted that the image is effaced, that man's affinity for God has been completely obliterated. While in his sin man is in flight from the eternal, his longing for the eternal persists; and he is never completely powerless to respond to God. Indeed, could God have led the Israelites to the Promised Land if they had not been able to heed His commands? Could Moses have become the leader of the Chosen People apart from his response to divine guidance? The testimony of Scripture does not say that man is so absolutely depraved that he is entirely separated from God.[2] St. Paul, while admitting that men "became futile in their thinking and their senseless minds were darkened," vigorously contends that the "law is written on the hearts of men" and that "their conscience also bears witness and their conflicting thoughts accuse or perhaps excuse." The apostle seems to be fully convinced that man is never without at least a modicum of goodness which calls him back to God. In summary, it can be said that the Biblical affirmation concerning man's affinity for God is this: Man, in his iniquity, is disobedient, forever falling short of fulfilling

God's commands. Yet, the dialogue between God and man persists, for, even in his worst perversity, man's consciousness of the transcendence and righteousness of God is never obliterated.

Concerning the Incarnation: [3] the decisive figure in all Biblical faith is Jesus Christ, the one sent by God to reconcile man unto Himself. "For God so loved the world that he gave his only Son, that whoever believes in him should not perish but have eternal life." "The Word became flesh and dwelt among us, full of grace and truth." In Christ, God came into history. As Professor C. H. Dodd says, "The inconceivable had happened: history had become the vehicle of the eternal; the absolute was clothed with flesh and blood. Admittedly, it was a 'mystery,' to be understood by those who have eyes to see and ears to hear, by those to whom it is revealed 'not by flesh and blood, but by My Father in heaven.'" [4] The final truth which redeems man and the world was revealed once and for all, through the only "begotten Son," God incarnate in man, Jesus Christ.

The doctrine of the Incarnation testifies, among other things, to the interaction between the divine and the human. Jesus disavows any claim to pre-eminence based upon His own merit. He is the Christ because of the good which God worketh in him. "I am not come of myself," He is reported to have said. "The words that I say to you I do not speak on my own authority; but the Father who dwells in me does his works." It is God who is at work within Jesus, and what is of the divine must not be attributed to the human. Yet, it is no less true that there is the human response to God. "I always do what is pleasing to Him," says Jesus. "For this reason the Father loves me, because I lay down my life, that I may take it again. No one takes it from me, but I lay it down of my own accord." There is no severance between the divine and the human; they touch each other, and there is communication between them. Jesus's life cannot be viewed apart from the response which He made to God's demands. Like all men, He was tempted to do evil, but unlike all men, He was without sin. Yet, His innocence must not be attributed to a mechanical power or an arbitrarily imposed goodness which precludes the possibility of sin. The temptation was real and His resistance involved self-discipline. "Although he was a Son, he learned obedience through what he suffered; and being made perfect, he became the source of eternal salvation." Yet, paradoxically enough, this does not mean that His sinlessness was not by the grace of God. "And he who sent me is with me; he has not left me alone." In the Incarnation we see God coming to man, and, at the same time, we see man seeking God. It is not a case of either the divine or the human, but of both.

The *eschaton* also shows the intercourse of God and man. According to Biblical eschatology the Transcendent God has already made himself known through Jesus Christ so that men now know—though through a glass darkly—of the Kingdom of God. In other words, the Kingdom of which the Bible speaks, has already come; it is presently known, and is among us. The power and glory of God has been revealed in Jesus Christ; God, through Christ, is at work in the world bringing both judgment and mercy. In this sense, the *eschaton* is already realized. But this is only part of the story; the other part is that the *eschaton* is yet to come. As a contemporary theologian says, the world awaits "a final consummation, a final judgment, an End which is 'not yet,' an eternal order of blessedness in God of which our Christian life in time is the foretaste and the firstfruits." [5] So the Kingdom, which is a present experience, awaits a future consummation.

Central to the eschatological hope is the doctrine of the Resurrection; in fact, the doctrine is central to the entire Christian faith. "For if the dead are not raised," writes St. Paul, "then Christ has not been raised. If Christ has not been raised, your faith is futile and you are still in your sins." Without the Resurrection there would be no Christianity. The Christian doctrine of the resurrection must be distinguished from the Greek idea of immortality. According to Hellenic thought, the human spirit is good and immortal while the body is evil and mortal. Accordingly, as they reason, man's essential nature is realized only as the soul is extricated from the body. Put in a broader context, immortality means the negation of the natural, the historical, the worldly, in order that the supernatural, the nonhistorical, the otherworldly may be realized. The idea of immortality, in other words, carries the assertion that there is a radical discontinuity between man's eternal nature and his historical existence. In the Christian hope of the resurrection this is not the case. The belief in the "resurrection of the dead" embodies the affirmation that eternal life is the fulfillment, and not the negation, of man's infinite, natural, historical existence. It asserts that there is a continuity between the "old" and the "new." It claims, in effect, that it is the entire self, not alone the soul, which is redeemed. St. Paul states that "flesh and blood cannot inherit" eternal life; yet, he did not thereby believe that the finite, natural existence of man is finally annulled. The "body" of the resurrected man will be one which is peculiar to the "celestial" rather than the "terrestrial" life. Again, the apostle, suggesting that eternal life is the completion, not the denial, of human life, says that the body will not be "unclothed" but will be "further clothed."

The eschatological hope, in its essential meaning, affirms that eternal life is not simply the judgment against man's existence, but is the fulfillment of it. When the "last things" shall occur, Christ shall come again to "judge the quick and the dead." Before the final word of God the proud imaginations and contrivings of the human spirit shall be brought low—the "old being" and the "old age" shall be shattered. At the same time, the present longings of the human spirit shall be fulfilled in the life eternal—the "New Being" and the "New Age" shall come to pass. That which men know in part and which is always corrupted by human pride will then be known face to face. The Book of Revelation speaks of "a new heaven and a new earth," of "the holy city, new Jerusalem." Commenting on this Scripture, St. Augustine says: "For when the judgment is finished, this heaven and earth shall cease to be, and there will be a new heaven and a new earth. For this world shall pass away by transmutation, not by absolute destruction." [6] The *eschaton*, like the *imago Dei* and the Incarnation, points to the fact that the human and the divine are inextricably related and that both must be taken seriously.

In these three Christian affirmations are contained several fundamental principles of the Christian faith which can be ignored only at the cost of distorting the gospel. They clearly assert that God is a transcendent God, the Lord of all life, the One who creates and loves all men and to whom all men are ultimately responsible. All things are of God, and it is through

Him, not through man himself, that the "whence" and "wherefore" of man's existence is established. Man is not an autonomous being, one who is able to give an explanation of and justification for his own existence. According to the Christian faith, any attempt to provide an account of man apart from the preeminent and initial fact of the sovereignty and love of God is a futile enterprise. God creates man; He redeems man; He gives man eternal life.

Yet, although the transcendental nature of God is a supreme fact, it must not be concluded that the Almighty works independently of man's concerns and endeavors; God is not severed from the struggles and thoughts and works of man. The Biblical statements make it clear that there is always a dialogue between God and man. Man never becomes either so intellectually astute or so spiritually evil that the connection between the divine and the human is completely broken. That man cries for the Eternal and that God acts in man's behalf and that there is interaction between the one and the Other—this belief is at the very core of the Christian idea of the *"imago Dei,"* the Incarnation and the *eschaton.*

Granted the above interpretation of Biblical faith, what can be said regarding the ideas which have been advanced by Fromm, Bonhoeffer, Schleiermacher, Barth, and Niebuhr? What kind of polemic have they set forth? In presenting the faith against the background of the Enlightenment, have they allowed the humanism of the eighteenth century to supersede the Christian faith? Or have they so delineated the Christian faith that they have estranged the gospel from the longings and needs of the human spirit? Or have they remained true to the essential meaning of the faith? The response to these ques-

[170]

tions falls into three groups: that of Fromm and Schleierma-cher, of Bonhoeffer and Barth, and of Niebuhr.

It appears that the ideas of both Fromm and Schleierma-cher have so emphasized the human that the divine is without crucial importance; the Christian accentuation of the transcend-ent and sovereign God is silenced, in deference to the human-ists' sounding praises to man. In Fromm's thought this fact is ex-plicitly evident. In Schleiermacher's thought it is somewhat hidden but, nevertheless, present. For Schleiermacher the Christian faith—which is an extension of religion—is a pos-sibility immanent in man himself. Professor H. L. Stewart could perhaps be accused of caricature when he remarked that "liberal theology [of the Schleiermacherian type] tended to reduce Faith to something little more than the genial human-ism of a service club." [7] Yet, this statement is not without a measure of truth. Wittingly or unwittingly, the ingredients of Schleiermacher's theology are primarily human rather than divine; his focal point is mainly man, not God. "Immediate consciousness, the movement of the soul within itself, the feel-ing of dependence"—because these experiences of the human heart represent what Schleiermacher conceives to be the essence of piety, and because he fails to take seriously—and perhaps this was his most crucial failing—the revelation in Jesus Christ, it seems that for him the primal and constant locus of faith is man himself.

Now in view of the fact that the religion of Fromm and Schleiermacher is essentially man-centered, it suffers from at least one serious infirmity. And in order to recognize this in-firmity we need to recall the criticisms that were hurled against religion by Karl Marx and Sigmund Freud. Marx argued that religion is nothing more than "an ideological superstructure" of man's economic desires and struggles; religion, he contended, is an "opiate of the people." And Freud insisted that religion is only a manifestation of man's wish for a father-protector: as the weak and helpless infant desires a father so the adult wishes for the existence of a god; religion, says Freud, is a psychic necessity. (When Freud observed the religious scene in America several decades ago he commented: "That the effect of the consolations of religion may be compared to that of a narcotic is prettily illustrated by what is happening in America. There they are now trying—plainly under the influence of petticoat government—to deprive men of all stimulants, intoxicants and luxuries [i.e., tea, alcohol, and tobacco], and to satiate them with piety by way of compensation." [8]) Are not both Fromm and Schleiermacher vulnerable to the attacks of Marx and Freud? If the basis for religion is grounded in man himself, can religion be anything other than a mirroring of human works and a projection of human wishes? Can truth and falsity, good and evil, be anything other than that which man wants them to be? Humanistic religious orientations are invariably betrayed by their own subjectivism.

Fromm explicitly denies that his "humanistic ethics"—i.e., his religion—can be regarded as a form of subjectivism. In fact, he openly disavows all subjectivism and points the finger at Freud for fathering a psychological approach to reality which is essentially relativistic. According to Freud's scheme of things, Fromm says, the content of conscience is nothing more than "a part of the system of commands and prohibitions embodied in the father's Super-Ego and the cultural tradition." [9] And Fromm goes on to say that what disassociates him from Freud's

[172]

error is that he (Fromm) employs the scientific method: Science, because it is based on the objective method, disallows all subjectivism.

But, the question arises, has Fromm actually proven his point? Is he really emancipated from all subjectivism? Does he not err in his failure to acknowledge that science itself is predicated on certain nonscientific presuppositions, on certain judgments of value? Professor A. D. Ritchie, an eminent English scholar, has written a book, *Scientific Method*, in which he states:

The man of science and his common sense forerunners brush aside a vast number of perplexing problems when they decide to disregard metaphysics and go straight to work on particular parts of the physical world. Their conception of the physical world is already saturated with metaphysics and metaphysics of the most dangerous sort, unconscious metaphysics inherited from our forebears or worked out in extreme youth. Lurking in the background of any description of what we see and touch and hear is some theory and some assumption as to the nature of things, the scientific man's escape from metaphysics is largely illusory.[10]

And in keeping with Ritchie's statement, Christopher Dawson explains in his *Religion and Culture* that the person of today who pretends to establish his religious position through the objective method of science is in fact involved in at least two nonscientific assumptions: ". . . the intimate relation that exists between the naturalistic theories of evolutionary development current since the nineteenth century, and the strictly idealistic conception of an inevitable progress of perfection which is a manifestation of the progressive self-realization of the absolute spirit of history."[11]

[173]

Despite claims to the contrary, the thought of both Fromm and Schleiermacher serves to aid and abet religion which is, in lieu of a determinative objective reality, fundamentally subjective. A place having been granted for the human dimension, which is, Biblically speaking, an aspect of the spiritual life, this dimension has been so exaggerated as to exclude the transcendent element, which is also essential to true faith. Thus both Fromm and Schleiermacher contribute to the support of the idea that that which is the proper focus of man's worship evolves out of man's own experience. For Fromm this focus consists of the values found in man himself. And in Schleiermacher's thought there is a tendency to put a premium on religion *per se*. The criterion for life is that which is subjectively discovered rather than that which is objectively given. There is a sense in which the "gods"—whatever forms they may take —of Fromm and Schleiermacher are not unlike the god of Brigitte Pian in Mauriac's *Woman of the Pharisees:* she "attributed to our Father in Heaven the complexities and perversities of her own nature." [12] The "gods" are being made in the image of man. Indeed, are not Fromm and Schleiermacher in part responsible for helping to bring about the kind of condition described by Cardinal Hamilcar von Schestedt—in Isak Dinesen's *The Deluge of Norderney:* " 'I am convinced,' he declared, 'that there has been a fall, but I do not hold that it is man who has fallen. I believe that there has been a fall of the divinity. We are now serving an inferior dynasty of heaven. . . . There are traditions still,' he went on, 'from *le Grand Monarque* and *le Grand Siècle*. But no human being with a feeling for greatness can possibly believe that the God who created the stars, the sea, and the desert, the poet Homer and the giraffe, is the same God who is now making, and upholding, the King of Belgium, the Poetical School of Schwaben, and the moral ideas of our day. . . . We are serving Louis Philippe, a human God, much as the King of France is a bourgeois King.' " [13]

At this point, the critics of the recent religious resurgence in America seem to be screaming for attention. Is not the subjectivism inherent in the thought of Fromm and Schleiermacher also contaminating the contemporary expressions of piety? Professor Richard Niebuhr takes us to the heart of the matter when he says: "The term 'religionist' which has been invented in modern times applies aptly to those who follow the tendency inaugurated in part by Schleiermacher, for religion is the object of concern and the source of strength for them rather than God whom an active faith regards as alone worthy of supreme devotion." [14] Is our ostensible worship of God, ask the critics, really anything more than the worship of ourselves, or, what is the same, the worship of the idea of worshiping? Is the prevailing piety throughout the country anything more than an outward expression of the subjective thoughts and ambitions of man? Is it not true that we have discarded the God who was revealed through Jesus Christ and replaced Him with the idols of this world? Professor Robert Brown seems to be painfully right when he asserts that "the tenuous religion to which we [Americans] have returned looks suspiciously like a gimmick for getting what we want." [15] Like the religion of Fromm and Schleiermacher, the "spiritual revival" of the day seems to be grounded more in man than in God.

Bonhoeffer and Barth are at strong odds with Fromm and Schleiermacher; while the former are not in total agreement with each other, they stand together in their opposition to the humanistic perspective of the latter. Both Bonhoeffer and Barth subscribe to the fundamental Christian affirmation that God is a transcendent reality and that He has revealed Himself through Jesus Christ. In this emphasis it is clear that their positions are not without a degree of Biblical basis. As theologians speaking within the classical Christian tradition, they will not subscribe to an explanation of the gospel which permits the Eternal elements of the gospel to be absorbed by human elements. Barth has been especially adamant on this matter, and, as Reinhold Niebuhr reminds us, we must "not forget to pay tribute to Barth's influence in the Anglo Saxon world in extricating the Christian faith from the idolatries of our day." [16]

Yet, Barth's inestimable contribution to contemporary theology must not blind us to the aberrant element of his exposition of the Christian faith. I am referring to his tendency to transcendentalize God to such an extent that the Christian faith has become virtually irrelevant to the human world. From the housetops Barth shouts: "God is in heaven and thou art on earth." And in effect what he is saying is that God is so completely transcendent that He has nothing to do with man. In Barth's theology, God is severed from human thoughts and endeavors: Historically, the Christian faith has nothing to offer to the world—it can say nothing about economics and politics. The Christian simply rejoices in a "revolutionary hope." Psychologically, man is without any capacity to be aware of God; man can do nothing about his salvation—absolutely nothing. God is so remote from man that man must go it alone. Barth acknowledges the fact, it is true, that Christ came into the world. But how is this event to be interpreted? "For Barth," Paul Tillich explains, "Christ appears in history in so far as he is above history; he does not participate in the developments of human history and of human spiritual life, but is God's insert into history." [17] Barth's theology represents a religious schizophrenia: since God is other than the world, God and the world are mutually exclusive. Is there not a striking affinity between Barth's theology and the popular piety "pie in the sky, by and by," and of the traditional "otherworldliness" motif? His "neo-orthodoxy" bears many of the overtones of contemporary orthodoxy, which insists that the Christian faith is concerned with man's personal salvation but that it has nothing to do with worldly enterprises of man's life. In Barth's theology, Reinhold Niebuhr reminds us, the Christian faith degenerates into a determination and irresponsibility wherein "the divine grace is regarded as a way of escape from, rather than a source of engagement with, the anxieties, perplexities, sins and pretensions of human existence." [18]

Bonhoeffer, unlike Barth, does not dwell so exclusively on the transcendent God as to sever the Eternal from the human. While he affirms the sovereignty of God, he retains—at least so it first appears—the idea of God's relevance to man. With unquestioning assurance, Bonhoeffer asserts that the Christian faith is always expressed through a worldly life. There can be no faith apart from worldliness. And by worldliness is meant "taking life in one's stride, with all its duties and problems, its successes and failures, its experiences and helplessness. It is in such a life that we throw ourselves utterly in the arms of God and participate in his sufferings in the world and watch with Christ in Gethsemane." [19] For Bonhoeffer, God is infinitely concerned about the life of man, and, thus, the Christian is one who identifies himself with the concerns of his fellow men. Herein lies God's relevance to the human world.

At the same time, Bonhoeffer's theology, like Barth's, tends to disassociate God from man. Bonhoeffer's thesis is that modern man is religionless. By this contention he means that man is not really "ultimately concerned" about his existence but feels self-sufficient, capable of determining his own destiny. Certainly, Bonhoeffer's description of the self-sufficiency of modern man must not be cavalierly laughed out of court. Will Herberg, who heartily disagrees with Bonhoeffer's main thesis, has presented some facts in his *Protestant-Catholic-Jew* which strongly suggest that throughout the prosperous and relatively serene United States there seems to be a conspicuous absence of existential anxiety and fear.[20] Also, Robin M. Williams, in his *American Society,* records the observation that in America the theology "that stressed original sin, the innate depravity of man, and the evils of the world and the flesh" has given way to a "resolute self-confidence and optimism" which have been ushered in by, among other things, "the objective situation of a wealthy, strong and expanding society." [21]

Yet, while Bonhoeffer's point of view is not bereft of all truth, it must be treated with certain reservations. Granted that since the Renaissance and the Enlightenment man has manifested a sense of self-sufficiency, and, granted too, that the traditional question of "saving one's soul" has become for many a rather inane affair, does it follow that man is unconcerned about the ultimate "whence" and "wherefore" of his life? Does man no longer ask the "life and death" questions of his existence?

The harassed Biblical character Job wanted to know, "If a man die, shall he live again?" [22] Pascal declared, "Nothing is so important to man as his own state, nothing is so formidable to him as eternity; and thus it is not natural that there should be men indifferent to the loss of their existence, and to the perils of everlasting suffering." [23] Koheleth, the reputed author of Ecclesiastes, was confounded by the fact "that the fate of the sons of men and the fate of beasts is the same; as one dies, so dies the other." [24] Calvin wrote in his *Institutes:* "Even those who in other respects appear to differ but little from brutes, always retain some sense of religion; so fully are the minds of men possessed with this common principle, which is closely interwoven with their original composition." [25] And Luther is in agreement with Calvin. Indeed, Professor Alexander Miller's suggestion (Chapter 3) that the religionless Christianity of Bonhoeffer is an expression of Luther's doctrine of "justification by Faith" is a case of forcing the reformer's theology into the Procrustean bed. There is a serious difference between the two. Bonhoeffer's basic assumption is that man is without religion whereas Luther, while declaring that in faith man transcends the religious concern, proceeds on the assumption that the Christian faith becomes intelligible only as it takes seriously the religious struggles and yearnings of man. In fact, as Roland Bainton reminds us, Luther's own "rebellion originated in an anguished concern as to his own status with God." [26] So for Luther, too, man is religious. All of these voices —Pascal, Koheleth, and the others—may be from the past, but one must disregard much of modern man's fear and anxiety to conclude that they are completely out of date.

It should be noted here that in looking for evidence to

support the idea that man is religionless some persons have turned to Camus. As a matter of fact, not a few contemporary theologians have insisted that Camus is in complete agreement with Bonhoeffer on this point. But this is a misrepresentation of Camus' thought. Camus' description of the human predicament does not assume Bonhoeffer's assertion that modern man is nonreligious—"Godless?" yes, but not "nonreligious." This is not the time for a lengthy discussion of this issue, nor is it necessary. The point can be quickly clarified. Bonhoeffer's contention is that man is nonreligious in that he is not ultimately concerned about his existence, an attitude which means, among other things, that man is not anxious about his "guilt and death." And all theologians, as well as existential philosophers, says Bonhoeffer, who assume that man is shaking in his boots because he is acutely aware of the absurdity of life and confounded by the inevitability of death have not taken seriously the fact that man has "come of age"—that man is "religionless." In the face of this statement, how can it be said that Bonhoeffer and Camus are in the same camp? Camus, in *The Myth of Sisyphus,* for example, depicts man as one who is existentially conscious of being an "alien," a "stranger" "in a universe suddenly divested of illusions and lights. . . . His exile is without remedy since he is deprived of the memory of a lost home or the hope of a promised land." [27] Man is yearning, anxious—religious. Camus does not support Bonhoeffer's position. Indeed, if we accept Bonhoeffer's definition of "religionlessness," we can rightly conclude that Camus is really a witness to contemporary man's religiousness.

Moreover, concerning Bonhoeffer's claim that man is religionless, it can be argued that if man is self-sufficient and is

[180]

unconcerned about his existence, how could he take seriously the commandment that he ought to identify himself with the sufferings of the world? For if man is completely satisfied with his existence would not the admonition that he ought to suffer in Gethsemane evoke only a contented yawn? Will a man take the road to martyrdom or will he even endure hardship and discomfort if he is unconcerned about the "whence" and "wherefore" of his existence? Apart from a religious concern, where is the precondition, the point of contact, whereby the commandment to suffer can take hold of man? If man has "given up worshipping everything, even idols" and if all men are "absolute nihilists," what would be the grounds for assuming that man would or could take seriously the "incarnation, cross and resurrection" of Jesus and the "new life for others"? Is it not a case of Bonhoeffer's tripping over his own feet when he assumes that man, because of his religiousness, cannot take seriously the matter of salvation but that he can take seriously the Being of Christ—the Christ who suffered in Gethsemane?

Both Barth and Bonhoeffer have propounded a theology which tends to separate God from man, although for different reasons. Barth, it seems, makes God irrelevant by accentuating the transcendence of God, while Bonhoeffer is on the verge of making God irrelevant by disassociating Him from the existential concerns of man's existence.

By the logic of the argument thus far, the suggestion naturally follows that Niebuhr's theology most nearly approximates the Biblical expression of the relation of faith to religion. His theology is basically a dialectical one, wherein there is a genuine encounter and interaction between the divine and the human. There is a continuous dialogue between God and man;

yet, God is always God and man is always man. Niebuhr takes seriously the Biblical affirmation concerning the transcendence of God. He acknowledges the fact that the Alpha and Omega of all life is the Almighty and Holy God. In keeping with the historic Christian affirmation, God, as revealed in Jesus Christ, is represented as the ultimate Word whereby the life of man can be understood and justified. In taking this stand, Niebuhr's theology is spared from the subjectivism contained in the thought of Fromm and Schleiermacher. He vigorously insists that God is the Lord of all life and that the divine must never be confused with the processes of history or be identified with man himself. The ultimate truth and goodness which all men seek, but from which they are estranged, comes to man by the grace of God, not through the ingenuity of the finite mind or the virtue of the human heart. True piety, true faith, is a gift of the Almighty and Loving God of the Old and New Testaments. Niebuhr takes seriously the Christian affirmations that God creates man in His image; that in Christ God comes to man; and that only through an act of God is man's life fulfilled.

Yet, while taking seriously the transcendent God, Niebuhr's theology does not disassociate God from the strivings and hopes of man. In keeping with the *imago Dei*, the Incarnation, and the *eschaton*, Niebuhr contends that man is forever reaching toward God and that ultimately the longings of the human spirit will be fulfilled. Man is unceasingly searching for truth and goodness, and in his searching he is in communion with God. The Almighty is not removed from man as Barth adamantly insists and as Bonhoeffer quietly suggests. The mighty acts of God must not be viewed apart from the efforts of man,

[182]

feeble though they be. In the religious concerns of man there is a point of contact between God and man, resulting in a dialectical relationship between the two.

Thus it appears that in delineating the Christian faith under the impact of the spirit of the eighteenth-century Enlightenment, Reinhold Niebuhr, of all the persons considered in this study, expressed the point of view which is most compatible with the essential meaning of the Biblical faith. In his insistence upon the dialectical relation between the divine and the human, he avoids, on the one hand, the irrelevancy of faith which is peculiar to the theology of Bonhoeffer and Barth and, on the other hand, the subjectivism of religion which is characteristic of the thought of Fromm and Schleiermacher. Niebuhr's theology provides the most adequate guide for understanding and evaluating the various manifestations of man's religious consciousness—and the various expressions of the Christian faith.

NOTES

Chapter 1. Introduction

1. Will Herberg, *Judaism and Modern Man* (Philadelphia: The Jewish Publication Society of America, 1951), p. 27.

2. Soren Kierkegaard, *The Sickness Unto Death*, trans. Walter Lowrie (Princeton: Princeton University Press, 1951), p. 83.

3. Leo Tolstoy, *Ivan Ilych and Hadji Murad*, trans. Louise and Aylmer Maude (New York: Oxford University Press, 1951), p. 3.

4. Paul Tillich, *Systematic Theology* (Chicago: University of Chicago Press, 1951), I, pp. 11–12.

5. J. S. Whale, *Christian Doctrine* (New York: The Macmillan Company, 1947), p. 14.

6. Crane Brinton, *Ideas and Men: The Story of Western Thought* (New York: Prentice-Hall, Inc., 1950), p. 258.

7. Crane Brinton, *A History of Western Morals* (New York: Harcourt, Brace & World, Inc., 1959), p. 297.

8. Brinton, *Ideas and Men*, p. 376.

9. Daniel A. Poling, "Dr. Poling Answers Your Questions,"

Christian Herald (Jan., 1956), p. 16; Poling, "Editorially Speaking . . . ," *Christian Herald* (June, 1957), pp. 4 ff.; "Selling Salvation," *The Economist* (Aug. 3, 1957), pp. 383–384; and Barbara Ward, "Report to Europe on America," *The New York Times Magazine* (June 20, 1954), pp. 7 ff.

10. ". . . Is our Religious Revival Real?" *McCall's Magazine* (June, 1955), p. 25.

11. Will Herberg, *Protestant-Catholic-Jew: An Essay in American Religious Sociology* (New York: Doubleday and Company, Inc., 1955), p. 276.

12. William L. Miller, "Piety Along the Potomac," *The Reporter* (Aug. 17, 1954), pp. 25–28.

Chapter 2. Religion Without the Christian Faith: Erich Fromm

1. Erich Fromm, *Man for Himself* (New York: Holt, Rinehart and Winston, Inc., 1947), p, 46.

2. Reinhold Niebuhr, *The Nature and Destiny of Man* (New York: Charles Scribner's Sons, 1951), I, pp. 150–177.

3. Ludwig Feuerbach, *The Essence of Christianity*, trans. Marian Evans (Boston: Houghton Mifflin Company, 1881), pp. 2–3.

4. Fromm, *Man for Himself*, p. 40.

5. Erich Fromm, *The Sane Society* (New York: Holt, Rinehart and Winston, Inc., 1955), p. 24.

6. Fromm, *Man for Himself*, p. 41.

7. *Ibid.*, p. 42.

8. Erich Fromm, *Escape from Freedom* (New York: Holt, Rinehart and Winston, Inc., 1941), Chap. V.

9. Fromm, *The Sane Society*, p. 25.

10. Fromm, *Man for Himself*, p. 19.

11. *Ibid.*, pp. 19–20.

12. John Dewey, *A Common Faith* (New Haven: Yale University Press, 1934), p. 31.

13. Fromm, *Man for Himself*, p. 24.

14. *Ibid.*, p. 229.

15. *Ibid.*, p. 97.

16. *Ibid.*, pp. 98–103.

17. *Ibid.*, pp. 103–105.

18. *Ibid.*, p. 107.

19. *Ibid.*, pp. 72–73.

20. *Ibid.*, p. 10.

21. *Ibid.*, p. 13.

22. *Ibid.*, p. 159.

23. Cited by Fromm in *Escape from Freedom*, p. 75, trans. Fromm.

24. Cited by Fromm in *Escape from Freedom*, pp. 84–85, beginning with the words "For, as it is . . ." the translation is Erich Fromm's from the Latin original, *Johannes Calvini Institutio Christianae Religionis*, Editionem curavit A. Tholuk, Beroloni, 1835, Part I, p. 445.

25. Fromm, *Escape from Freedom*, p. 81.

26. Fromm, *Man for Himself*, p. 211.

27. Cited by Fromm in *Escape from Freedom*, pp. 86, 85.

28. Cited by Fromm in *Escape from Freedom*, p. 75, trans. Fromm.

29. Cited by Fromm in *Escape from Freedom*, pp. 75–76.

30. Fromm, *Man for Himself*, p. 216.

31. *Ibid.*, p. 218.

32. *Ibid.*

33. Fromm, *Escape from Freedom,* p. 171.

34. Feuerbach, *The Essence of Christianity,* p. 184.

Chapter 3. *The Christian Faith Without Religion: Dietrich Bonhoeffer*

1. Dietrich Bonhoeffer, *The Cost of Discipleship,* trans. Reginald H. Fuller (New York: The Macmillan Company, 1948), p. 193.

2. *Ibid.,* p. 194.

3. Dietrich Bonhoeffer, *Life Together,* trans. John W. Doberstein (New York: Harper & Brothers, 1954), p. 22.

4. Dietrich Bonhoeffer, *Prisoner for God: Letters and Papers in Prison,* ed. Eberhard Bethge, trans. Reginald H. Fuller (New York: The Macmillan Company, 1954), p. 122.

5. *Ibid.,* p. 146.

6. *Ibid.*

7. *Ibid.,* pp. 146–147.

8. Cited by Roger Hazelton in "Was Nietzsche an Anti-Christian?", *Journal of Religion* (Jan., 1942), p. 67.

9. Bonhoeffer, *Prisoner for God,* p. 148.

10. *Ibid.,* pp. 122–123, 126, 148.

11. *Ibid.,* pp. 147–148.

12. *Ibid.,* p. 153.

13. Rudolf Bultmann, *Kerygma and Myth: A Theological Debate,* ed. Hans Werner Batsch, trans. Reginald H. Fuller (New York: The Macmillan Company, 1953), p. 3.

14. Bonhoeffer, *Prisoner for God,* p. 149.

15. Rudolf Bultmann, *Essays,* trans. James C. G. Greig

(New York: The Macmillan Company, 1955), pp. 136–137. See also Bultmann's *Kerygma and Myth: A Theological Debate*, pp. 28–29.

16. Bonhoeffer, *Prisoner for God*, p. 147.

17. *Ibid.*, pp. 123–124.

18. *Ibid.*, p. 167.

19. *Ibid.*, p. 169.

20. (Garden City, New York: Doubleday and Company, Inc., 1955), p. 72.

21. *Ibid.*, p. 73.

22. Bonhoeffer, *Prisoner for God*, p. 184.

23. Ed. Eberhard Bethge (New York: The Macmillan Company, 1955), p. 56.

24. *Ibid.*, p. 9.

25. *Ibid.*

26. *Ibid.*, p. 10.

27. Dietrich Bonhoeffer, "Concerning the Christian Idea of God," *The Journal of Religion* (April, 1932), p. 185.

28. Bonhoeffer, *Ethics*, pp. 94–95.

29. Bonhoeffer, *Prisoner for God*, p. 163.

30. *Ibid.*, p. 124.

31. *Ibid.*, p. 153.

32. *Ibid.*, p. 124.

33. *Ibid.*, p. 126.

34. *Ibid.*, p. 167.

35. *Ibid.*, p. 164.

36. *Ibid.*, p. 179.

37. *Ibid.*, p. 169.

38. *Ibid.*, p. 166.

39. *Ibid.*, p. 180.

Chapter 4. The Christian Faith as the Fulfillment of Religion: Friedrich Schleiermacher

1. Immanuel Kant, *Kant's Critique of Practical Reason and Other Works on the Theory of Ethics,* trans. Thomas K. Abbott (London: Longmans, Green & Company, 4th ed., rev., 1889), p. 47.

2. Robert M. Wernaer, *Romanticism and the Romantic School in Germany* (New York: D. Appleton and Company, 1910), pp. 12–13.

3. *Ibid.,* p. 145.

4. Friedrich Schleiermacher, *On Religion: Speeches to its Cultured Despisers,* trans. John Oman (London: Kegan Paul, Trench, Trübner and Co., 1893), p. 4.

5. *Ibid.,* pp. 15–16.

6. *Ibid.,* p. 36.

7. *Ibid.,* p. 15.

8. Friedrich Schleiermacher, *The Christian Faith,* ed. H. R. Mackintosh and J. S. Stewart (Edinburgh: T. and T. Clark, 1956), p. 78.

9. *Ibid.,* pp. 10–11.

10. Hugh Ross Mackintosh, *Types of Modern Theology* (London: Nisbet and Co., Ltd., 1947), p. 46.

11. Rudolph Otto, *Religious Essays: A Supplement to 'The Idea of the Holy,'* trans. Brian Lunn (London: Oxford University Press, 1931), p. 75.

12. Schleiermacher, *The Christian Faith,* p. 52.

13. *Ibid.,* p. 68.

14. *Ibid.,* p. 431.

15. *Ibid.*, p. 361.

16. *Ibid.*, p. 58.

17. *Op. cit.*, pp. 88–89.

18. Schleiermacher, *The Christian Faith*, p. 385.

19. *Ibid.*, p. 381.

20. William Adams Brown, *Chrisitan Theology in Outline* (New York: Charles Scribner's Sons, 1906), pp. 346–347.

21. Schleiermacher, *The Christian Faith*, p. 476.

22. *Ibid.*, pp. 17–18.

23. *Ibid.*, p. 476.

24. *Ibid.*

25. Shailer Mathews, "Doctrines of Social Patterns," *The Journal of Religion* (Jan., 1930) p. 7; *The Faith of Modernism* (New York: The Macmillan Company, 1924), p. 152.

26. Schleiermacher, *The Christian Faith*, p. 271.

27. *Ibid.*, p. 273.

28. *Ibid.*, p. 19.

29. *Ibid.*, pp. 564–565.

30. *Ibid.*, p. 247.

31. *Ibid.*, p. 17.

32. *Ibid.*, p. 12.

33. *Ibid.*, p. 17.

34. *Ibid.*, p. 16.

35. *Ibid.*, p. 201.

36. *Ibid.*, p. 76.

37. *Ibid.*, p. 194.

38. Phillips Brooks, "Need for Enthusiasm for Humanity," *National Needs and Remedies* (New York: Baker and Taylor Co., 1890), p. 306.

*Chapter 5. The Christian Faith as the Judgment
Against Religion: Karl Barth*

1. Karl Barth, *The Word of God and the Word of Man,*
trans. Douglas Horton (New York: Harper & Brothers, 1928),
p. 100.

2. Karl Barth, *Church Dogmatics,* ed. G. W. Bromiley
and T. F. Torrance, trans. G. T. Thomson and Harold Knight
(New York: Charles Scribner's Sons, 1956), I, Part 2, p. 282.

3. Karl Barth, *The Word of God and the Word of Man,*
pp. 195–196.

4. Karl Barth, *Protestant Thought: From Rousseau to
Ritschl,* trans. Brian Cozens (New York: Harper & Brothers,
1959), Chap. VIII.

5. Barth, *The Word of God and the Word of Man,* p. 246.

6. H. Emil Brunner, *The Theology of Crisis* (New York:
Charles Scribner's Sons, 1931), p. 6.

7. Quoted in R. Birch Hoyle, *The Teaching of Karl Barth*
(New York: Charles Scribner's Sons, 1930), p. 88.

8. *Ibid.,* p. 89.

9. Barth, *The Word of God and the Word of Man,* p. 246.

10. Albrecht Ritschl, *The Christian Doctrine of Justification and Reconciliation,* trans. H. R. Mackintosh and A. B.
Macauley (New York: Charles Scribner's Sons, 1900), p. 205.

11. Waldo Beach, "Christian Ethics," *Protestant Thought
in the Twentieth Century,* ed. Arnold Nash (New York: The
Macmillan Company, 1951), p. 128.

12. William Ralph Inge, "Harnack and Liberal Protestantism," *Hibbert Journal* (1927–1928), p. 634.

13. *Ibid.*

14. Barth, *The Word of God and the Word of Man,* pp. 240–241.

15. Karl Barth, *The Epistle to the Romans,* trans. Edwyn C. Hoskyns (New York: Oxford University Press, 1953), p. 10.

16. Barth, *Church Dogmatics,* I, Part 2, pp. 281–282.

17. *Ibid.,* p. 282.

18. Karl Barth, *Dogmatics in Outline,* trans. G. T. Thomson (London: SCM Press, 1949), p. 37.

19. *Ibid.,* p. 36.

20. *Ibid.,* p. 23.

21. *Ibid.,* p. 68.

22. *Ibid.*

23. Barth, *Church Dogmatics,* I, Part 2, p. 31.

24. *Ibid.,* p. 172.

25. *Ibid.*

26. *Ibid.,* p. 301.

27. *Ibid.,* p. 302.

28. *Ibid.,* p. 308.

29. *Ibid.,* p. 309.

30. *Barth, Dogmatics in Outline,* p. 36.

31. Karl Barth, *The Knowledge of God and the Service of God According to the Teaching of the Reformation,* trans. J. L. M. Haire and Ian Henderson (London: Hodder and Stoughton), p. 50.

32. *Natural Theology: Comprising "Nature and Grace" by Professor Dr. Emil Brunner and the reply "No!" by Dr. Karl Barth,* trans. Peter Fraenkel (London: Geoffrey Bles: The Centenary Press, 1946), p. 70.

33. *Ibid.,* pp. 31, 17–35.

34. *Ibid.*, p. 71.

35. *Ibid.*, p. 105.

36. Cited by Barth in *Natural Theology*, p. 107.

37. Barth, *Church Dogmatics*, I, Part 2, p. 315.

38. *Ibid.*, p. 316.

39. *Ibid.*, pp. 318, 317–318.

40. *Ibid.*, p. 319.

41. *Ibid.*

42. *Ibid.*, pp. 319–320.

43. *Ibid.*, p. 322.

44. *Ibid.*, p. 327.

45. *Ibid.*, pp. 327–328.

46. *Ibid.*, p. 345.

47. *Ibid.*, pp. 358–359.

Chapter 6. The Christian Faith as the Judgment Against and the Fulfillment of Religion: Reinhold Niebuhr

1. Cited by Reinhold Niebuhr, *An Interpretation of Christian Ethics* (New York: Harper & Brothers, 1935), p. 170.

2. *Ibid.*

3. Adolf Harnack, *What is Christianity?*, trans. Thomas B. Saunders (New York: G. P. Putnam's Sons, 1901), p. 154.

4. *Ibid.*, p. 55.

5. Walter Rauschenbusch, *A Theology for the Social Gospel* (New York: The Macmillan Company, 1918), Chap. XIII.

6. *Reinhold Niebuhr: His Religious, Social, and Political Thought,* ed. Charles W. Kegley and Robert W. Bretall (New York: The Macmillan Company, 1957), II, p. 6.

7. Cited by Reinhold Niebuhr, *The Nature and Destiny of Man* (New York: Charles Scribner's Sons, 1951), I, p. 186.

8. Reinhold Niebuhr, "Is There a Revival of Religion?" *The New York Times Magazine* (Nov. 19, 1950), pp. 60–62.

9. Niebuhr, *The Nature and Destiny of Man*, I, p. 131.

10. Emil Brunner, *Revelation and Reason* (Philadelphia: The Westminster Press, 1946), p. 262.

11. Niebuhr, *An Interpretation of Christian Ethics*, p. 7.

12. *Ibid.*

13. Hans Hoffman, *The Theology of Reinhold Niebuhr*, trans. Louise Pettibone Smith (New York: Charles Scribner's Sons, 1956), p. 24.

14. *Ibid.*, p. 24; also, pp. 89 ff.

15. Niebuhr, *The Nature and Destiny of Man*, II, p. 35.

16. *Ibid.*, I, p. 142.

17. Romans 1:18.

18. Niebuhr, *The Nature and Destiny of Man*, I, p. 142.

19. Reinhold Niebuhr, *Faith and History* (New York: Charles Scribner's Sons, 1949), p. 144.

20. Niebuhr, *The Nature and Destiny of Man*, I, pp. 147–148.

21. Reinhold Niebuhr, *Beyond Tragedy* (New York: Charles Scribner's Sons, 1937), p. 14.

22. *Ibid.*

23. Niebuhr, *The Nature and Destiny of Man*, II, p. 62.

24. *Ibid.*, I, p. 146.

25. Schleiermacher, *On Religion*, p. 250.

26. Niebuhr, *The Nature and Destiny of Man*, I, p. 145.

27. Emil Brunner, *Revelation and Reason*, p. 264.

28. Niebuhr, *An Interpretation of Christian Ethics*, p. 67.

29. *Ibid.*, pp. 86–87.

30. Brunner, *Revelation and Reason*, p. 264.

31. Niebuhr, *The Nature and Destiny of Man*, I, p. 200.

32. Cited by Niebuhr in *The Nature and Destiny of Man*, I, p. 201.

33. Niebuhr, *The Nature and Destiny of Man*, I, pp. 200–201.

34. Herbert Butterfield, *Christianity and History* (New York: Charles Scribner's Sons, 1949), p. 88.

35. Cited by Niebuhr in *The Nature and Destiny of Man*, I, p. 267.

36. *Ibid.*, II, p. 63.

37. *Ibid.*

38. *Ibid.*

39. Niebuhr, *Faith and History*, p. 175.

40. *Ibid.*

41. Niebuhr, *The Nature and Destiny of Man*, I, p. 266.

42. *Ibid.*, II, p. 252.

43. *Ibid.*, p. 284.

44. *Ibid.*, p. 256.

45. *Ibid.*, p. 67.

Chapter 7. Conclusion

1. *The Confessions of St. Augustine*, trans. E. B. Pusey (New York: E. P. Dutton & Co., Inc., 1949), p. 220.

2. John Baillie, *The Idea of Revelation in Recent Thought* (New York: Columbia University Press, 1958), p. 68.

3. For the entire discussion on the nature of Jesus Christ, I have relied heavily upon John Baillie, *op. cit.*, pp. 69–70.

4. *The Parables of the Kingdom* (London: Nisbet and Co., 1952), p. 197.

5. J. S. Whale, *Christian Doctrine* (New York: The Macmillan Company, 1947), pp. 182–183.

6. *City of God*, trans. Marcus Dods (New York: The Modern Library, 1950), XX, 14, p. 732.

7. H. L. Stewart, "Schleiermacher, Ritschl, Barth," *The Hibbert Journal* (Oct. 1951), p. 17.

8. Sigmund Freud, *The Future of An Illusion*, trans. W. D. Robson-Scott (London: Hogarth Press, 1928), pp. 87–88.

9. Erich Fromm, *Man for Himself*, p. 34.

10. (New York: Harcourt, Brace & World, Inc., 1923), p. 6.

11. (New York: Sheed and Ward, 1948), p. 17.

12. Trans. Gerard Hopkins (New York: Farrar, Straus and Young, Inc., 1946), p. 24.

13. See *Seven Gothic Tales* (New York: The Modern Library, 1934), pp. 55–56.

14. H. Richard Niebuhr, *The Meaning of Revelation* (New York: The Macmillan Company, 1941), p. 28.

15. Cited by Bernard E. Meland in "This Upsurge of Faith," *The Christian Century* (May 11, 1955), p. 562.

16. Reinhold Niebuhr, "An Answer to Karl Barth," *The Christian Century* (Feb. 23, 1949), p. 234.

17. Paul Tillich, "What is Wrong with the 'Dialectic' Theology?" *The Journal of Religion* (Apr., 1935), p. 133.

18. Reinhold Niebuhr, "We are Men and Not God," *The Christian Century* (Oct. 27, 1948), p. 1140.

19. Dietrich Bonhoeffer, *Prisoner for God*, p. 169.

20. (New York: Doubleday and Company, Inc., 1956), pp. 85–86.

21. (New York: Alfred A. Knopf, Inc., 1951), pp. 328–329.

22. Job 14:14.

23. Blaise Pascal, *Pensees,* trans. W. F. Trotter (New York: E. P. Dutton & Co., Inc., 1948), p. 56.

24. Ecclesiastes 3:19.

25. John Calvin, *Institutes of the Christian Religion,* trans. John Allen, 7th American edition (Philadelphia: Presbyterian Board of Christian Education, 1928), I, p. 54.

26. *The Age of the Reformation* (New York: D. Van Nostrand Co., Inc., 1956), p. 49.

27. Albert Camus, *The Myth of Sisyphus and Other Essays,* trans. Justin O'Brien (New York: Alfred A. Knopf, Inc.), p. 6.

INDEX

Aeschylus, cited, 58

Age of Reason, 136; *see also* Enlightenment

Alembert, Jean le Rond d', cited, 81

Allwohn, Adolf, cited, 109

American Society (Williams), 178

Aquinas, Thomas, 44

Art of Loving, The (Fromm), 19

Atheism, 4, 126–127

Augustine, Saint, cited, 44, 47, 141, 156–157, 164, 169

Authoritarianism, 38–43

Avesta, 116

Bainton, Roland, cited, 179

Barth, Karl, 47, 49, 63–64, 105–106; on Schleiermacher, 106–107, 110–111; reaction against liberalism, 107–113;

Barth, Karl (*cont.*)
on Ritschl, 110, 111; theology of, 113–115, 175–181; on religion and Christian faith 115–116; on nature of God, 116–118; on nature of Jesus Christ, 117–120; thesis on Christian faith as judgment against religion, 117–128; debate with Brunner, 122; on mysticism, 125–126, 127; on atheism, 126–127; Niebuhr on, 156

Beach, Waldo, cited, 111

Bentham, Jeremy, 26

Berdayaev, Nicholas, cited, 4

Beyond Tragedy (Niebuhr), 134

Bonhoeffer, Dietrich, 49–50; traditional concepts of, 51–55; theological background, 52–55; influence of Enlighten-

Bonhoeffer, Dietrich (*cont.*)
ment on, 55–59; formation of
thesis of, 59–60; on nature of
man, 61–63; thesis of religionless Christianity, 61–69;
on Barth, 64; on Tillich, 64;
on Bultmann, 65; on nature
of Jesus Christ, 69–76; theology of, 175–181
Brinton, Crane, cited, 9
Brooks, Phillips, cited, 104
Brown, Robert, cited, 175
Brown, William Adams, cited,
80, 95
Brunner, Emil, 47, 80; cited,
108, 146, 151, 154; debate
with Barth, 122
Buddhists, 116
Bultmann, Rudolf, cited, 63–64
Butterfield, Herbert, cited, 155–
156

Calvin, John, 39, 42, 47, 85;
cited, 44, 113, 122–123, 179
Camus, Albert, 180
Celsus, 9
Christian faith: defined, 6–8; religion without, 20–21; authoritarian ethics of, 38–43;
as inimical to true religion,
47; Bonhoeffer's concept of,
51–55, 177–178; conflict with
humanism, 59–60; Barth's
concept of, 60–77, 177; Jesus

Christian faith (*cont.*)
Christ as basis for, 69–76;
Schleiermacher on need for
changes in presentation of,
83–84; as fulfillment of religion, 93, 156; as judgment
against religion, 117–128,
151–155; as true religion,
128–131; as judgment against
and fulfillment of religion,
135, 161–162; Niebuhr on,
141–144, 148, 181–183; affirmations of, 163–170
Christian Faith, The (Schleiermacher), 80, 93, 103
Christianity: since Enlightenment, 9–13; historic criticisms
against, 10–13 *passim; see
also* Christian faith
Christliche Welt, Die (Rade),
105
Church, The: Bonhoeffer on
role of, 76; Barth's criticism
of modern, 108–110
Clement, 9
Communism, 4
Condorcet, Marie Jean Antoine
Nicolas Caritat, marquis de,
cited, 22–23
Consciousness, 29–30
Cost of Discipleship, The (Bon-
hoeffer), 50
Creation, 7, 13
Critique of Pure Reason, The
(Kant), 87

Dawson, Christopher, cited, 173

Death, 31, 51

"Death of Ivan Ilych, The," (Tolstoy), 5

Delbrück, Hans, 49

Deluge of Norderney, The (Dinesen), 174–175

Descartes, René, 58, 107

Dewey, John, cited, 3, 33

Dinesen, Isak, cited, 174–175

Dodd, C. H., cited, 166

Dogmatics in Outline (Barth), 117

Dohnanyi, Hans von, 50

Eckhart, Roy, 16

Eisenhower, Dwight D., 14–17

Elson, Edward L. R., 15

Enlightenment, 9–13; influence on Christian faith, 21–27 *passim;* spirit of, in Fromm, 27–28; influence on Bonhoeffer, 55–59; influence on Schleiermacher, 81–86; Barth's reaction against, 107–110; Niebuhr on, 135, 136

Epistle to the Romans, The (Barth), 106

Erasmus, 45

Escape from Freedom (Fromm), 19, 43–44

Eschaton, 167–170

Ethics, 32–33; humanistic, 38–39; authoritarian, 38–43 pas-

Ethics (*cont.*)
 sim; Christian, 56–57; and liberal movement, 111–112

Ethics (Bonhoeffer), 70

Evil, 21, 44–46 *passim*, 97–98, 143–144; *see also* Sin

Existence, 28–32, 61–63, 145–147 *passim*, 164; *see also* Man; Religion

Faith, 54–55, 84; *see also* Christian faith

Feuerbach, Ludwig, cited, 29–30, 47

Ford, Henry, 140

Francke, August, 86

Freud, Sigmund, cited, 47, 171–172

Fromm, Erich, 19–20; on authoritarianism of Christianity, 8; on nature of religion, 20–21; on Spinoza, 27–28; thesis on nature of man and religion, 27–47; Bonhoeffer on, 51; humanism of, 171–175

Gemeinsames Leben (Bonhoeffer), 50

God: relationship to religion, 3–4; according to Christian faith, 7–8; Fromm on, 20, 40–43; Bonhoeffer's concept of, 52–53, 61–63, 73–74; Kant on knowledge of, 87–88; Romantic concept of, 89; Schlei-

God (*cont.*)

ermacher on nature of, 95–96, 100–103; Barth's concept of, 113–114, 116–118; as sole source of Christian religion, 129; Niebuhr's concept of, 141, 149–152, 181–183; image of, 163–166; Incarnation of, 166–167; transcendent, 167–170, 171, 176–177, 182; sovereignty of, 177–178

Government, 161

Grace, 128, 158

Graham, Billy, 14, 15

Harnack, Adolf von, 49, 133, 137–138

Helvetius, Claude Adrien, 22, 82

Herberg, Will, cited, 4, 16, 178

Herbert of Cherbury, Lord, cited, 56

Herrmann, Wilhelm, 105

History, man's involvement with, 32

Hoffman, Hans, cited, 148

Holbach, Paul Henri, Baron d', 82

Humanism, 20–28, 55–59, 107–108, 171–175

Hume, David, 26, 87

Immortality, 168

Incarnation, 166–167; *see also* Jesus Christ

Inge, William Ralph, quoted, 112

Institutes of the Christian Religion (Calvin), 42, 106, 179

Interpretation of Christian Ethics, An (Niebuhr), 134, 148

Jefferson, Thomas, cited, 136

Jesus Christ: role in Christianity, 7–8; Bonhoeffer on, 53–54, 67, 69–76; and Pietism, 86; Schleiermacher on nature of, 93–96, 99–100; Ritschl on, 112; Barth on nature of, 117–120; as Creator of Christian religion, 129; divinity of, 136; Harnack on, 137–138; Niebuhr on, 148–152; as God incarnate in man, 166–167

Justice, 160–161

Kant, Immanuel, 85, 87–88

Keyserling, Hermann, cited, 109

Kierkegaard, Soren, 5, 113–115, 141, 142

Kingdom of God, 7, 138, 139, 167–168

Kitschl, Albrecht, 80

Koheleth, 179

Kraemer, Hendrik, cited, 155

Lactantius, Lucius Caelius Firmianus, cited, 3

Liberalism, 105–107, 109–113, 136–139, 140–141

Lietzmann, Hans, 49
Life, 31; *see also* Existence
Locke, John, 24–25
Love, 8, 98–100, 140, 143, 149, 157–161
Luther, Martin, 39, 42, 43–45 *passim*, 47, 68–69, 85, 179
Lyman, Eugene, 80

Machiavelli, Niccolò, cited, 57–58
Mackintosh, H. R., cited, 92, 94
Man: nature of, 7, 11–12; as source of religion, 20–21, 104; fundamental goodness of, 21–23, 45–47; perfectibility of, 22–23; as source of morality, 25–27; Fromm on nature of, 30–32, 33–34, 44–46; involvement with history, 32; productivity of, 35–38; as autonomous being, 38; Bonhoeffer's concept of, 52, 61–63; Schleiermacher on nature of, 90, 97–100; awareness of God, 95–96; Barth on nature of, 113, 115–116, 117; Niebuhr on nature of, 141, 142, 152–153, 156–157; as religious being, 144–148; relationship to God, 163–170; *see also* Existence
Man for Himself (Fromm), 19
Marx, Karl, 171–172
Marxism, 4

Mathews, Shailer, cited, 80, 96
Mauriac, François, cited, 174
Miller, Alexander, cited, 68–69, 179
Miller, William L., cited, 16
Montaigne, Michel de, cited, 56–57
Morality, man as source of, 25–27
Moral Man and Immoral Society (Niebuhr), 134
Mysticism, 125–126, 127
Myth of Sisyphus, The (Camus), 180

Naturalism, 10–14 *passim*, 23–28, 122
Nature and Destiny of Man, The (Niebuhr), 134, 145
"Nature and Grace" (Brunner), 122
"New Testament and Mythology" (Bultmann), 65
Newton, Isaac, 23–24
Niebuhr, Reinhold, 29, 47, 133–134; influences on theology of, 135, 141–142; early liberalism of, 137–140; on Christian faith, 141–144; on religion, 144–148; on relationship of Christian faith to religion, 148; on Jesus Christ, 148–152; on Christian faith as judgment against religion, 151–155; on nature of man

Niebuhr, Reinhold (*cont.*)
and religion, 152–153, 156–158; on sinful pride, 154–155; on Christian faith as fulfillment of religion, 156; on relation of love and justice, 160–161; on Christian faith as judgment against and fulfillment of religion, 161–162; on term "religionist," 175; on Barth, 176, 177; theology of, 181–183
Nietzsche, Friedrich, 63
Nixon, Richard, 15
Novalis, cited, 89

On Religion (Schleiermacher), 80, 90, 103
Origen, 9
Otto, Rudolph, cited, 80, 92
Owen, Robert, cited, 21
Oxnam, G. Bromley, cited, 16

Pascal, Blaise, cited, 179
Patterson, Grove, 15
Paul, Saint, 47, 151
Peale, Norman Vincent, 14, 15
Pietism, 85–86
Poling, Daniel A., cited, 10, 15
Pope, Alexander, quoted, 25
Pride, 141, 142
Prisoner for God (Bonhoeffer), 66, 70, 75
Productiveness, 34–38

Prometheus, 58–59
Protagoras, cited, 33
Psychoanalysis, 34
Psychoanalysis and Religion (Fromm), 19

Rade, Martin, 105
Rationalism, 81–82, 85; *see also* Enlightenment
Rauschenbusch, Walter, cited, 139
Reason, 11, 23–25, 56, 84, 87–88; *see also* Enlightenment
Redemption, 93–94, 149
Reformation, 84–85; *see also* Calvin; Luther
Religion: defined, 3–6; in United States, 14–17; man as sole agent of, 20–21; founded on reason, 23–25; as human phenomenon, 28–29; existential basis of, 32; Christian faith without, 60–77; Pietist concept of, 86; Schleiermacher's interpretation of, 89–93; Barth on universality of, 115–116; Christian faith as judgment against, 116–128, 151–155; Niebuhr on, 134, 144–148; Christian faith as fulfillment of, 156; Christian faith as judgment against and fulfillment of, 161–162; Freud

Religion (*cont.*)
on, 171–172; Marx on, 171–172; humanistic, 174–175

Religion and Culture (Dawson), 173

Renewal of Man, The (Miller), 68

Resurrection, 168

Revelation, 11, 96, 104, 118–120, 123, 145–146

Righteousness, 54, 55

Ritchie, A. D., cited, 173

Ritschl, Albrecht, 111–112 *passim*

Romanticism, 85, 87–88

Rousseau, Jean Jacques, cited, 21

Salvation, 12–13, 54–55, 67–68, 72, 74, 113

Sayers, Dorothy L., cited, 118

Schestedt, Hamilcar von, cited, 174–175

Schlegel, Friedrich, cited, 89

Schleiermacher, Friedrich, 47, 79–80, 81; influences on theology of, 81–90; interpretation of religion, 89–93; on Christian faith as fulfillment of religion, 93, 104; on nature of Jesus Christ, 93–96, 99–100; on nature of man, 97–100; on nature of God, 100–103; Barth on, 106–107,

Schleiermacher, Friedrich (*cont.*)
110–111; cited, 151; humanism of, 171–175

Science, 23–25, 33–34, 65, 173

Scientific Method (Ritchie), 173

Seeberg, A., 49

Self-preservation, 34

Sin, 53–55 *passim*, 62, 72, 98, 100, 120, 129–130, 136, 141, 142, 154–155, 165; *see also* Evil

Social gospel, 136, 139

Spener, Philipp, 86

Spinoza, Baruch, 27–28

Stewart, H. L., cited, 171

Subjectivism, 172

Suffering, 75–76

Supernaturalism, 10–14 *passim*, 82

Tertullian, 9

Tillich, Paul, cited, 5–6, 63–64, 177

Tolstoy, Leo, cited, 5

Trinity, 136

Tripitaka, 116

Troeltsch, Ernest, 80

Truth, 123–124, 157–158

Turgot, Anne Robert Jacques, cited, 82

United States of America, religion, in, 14–17, 137–140, 172, 175

Veda, 116

Wernaer, Robert, cited, 88, 89

Whale, J. S., cited, 7

Williams, Robin M., cited, 178

Woman of the Pharisees (Mauriac), 174

Zinzendorf, Nikolaus Ludwig, Count von, 86